Shakespeare's Heartbeat

Children on the autistic spectrum experience varying degrees of difficulties; all of which can be understood as a disassociation of mind and body. Expressing feelings, making eye contact, keeping a steady heartbeat and recognizing faces are all part of the autism dilemma which can be explored through Shakespeare's plays, because of the wealth of his poetic definitions of seeing, thinking and loving.

Over ten years, Hunter worked with children on all points of the spectrum, developing drama games for the specific purpose of combating autism. *Shakespeare's Heartbeat* is a step-by-step guide, detailing how to demonstrate, play and share these sensory games. The book includes:

- games based on *A Midsummer Night's Dream* and *The Tempest*
- tips and advice for playing one-on-one with the children.

This book provides an indispensable learning tool for those wishing to encourage children's eye contact and facial expression, improve their spatial awareness and language skills and introduce them to imaginative play.

Kelly Hunter is an award-winning actor, director, and educator, who has worked with the Royal Shakespeare Company and the highly-acclaimed Vesturport. Her work with Shakespeare and autism forms the basis of a longitudinal study at Ohio State University.

Praise for this book

'This book makes an outstanding contribution to its field.'
Joe Winston, *University of Warwick, UK*

'The real value of this book is its compelling pedagogical account of learning about teaching and its complexities, alongside its important story of learning with and through drama and Shakespeare.'
Kathleen Gallagher, *University of Toronto, Canada*

'This book is a significant and valuable resource that offers an important extension of practical Shakespeare work into the field of applied performance. It provides an original approach to working with autistic children, as well as a new understanding of Shakespearean efficacy.'
Nicola Shaughnessy, *University of Kent, UK*

Shakespeare's Heartbeat

Drama games for children with autism

Kelly Hunter

Routledge
Taylor & Francis Group

LONDON AND NEW YORK

First published 2015
by Routledge
2 Park Square, Milton Park, Abingdon, Oxon OX14 4RN

and by Routledge
711 Third Avenue, New York, NY 10017

Routledge is an imprint of the Taylor & Francis Group, an informa business

British Library Cataloguing in Publication Data
A catalogue record for this book is available from the British Library

Library of Congress Cataloging-in-Publication Data
Hunter, Kelly (Educator)
Shakespeare's heartbeat: drama games for children with autism / by Kelly Hunter.
    pages cm
 1. Autistic children – Rehabilitation. 2. Drama – Therapeutic use.
 3. Shakespeare, William, 1564–1616 – Study and teaching (Elementary)
 I. Title.
 RJ506.A9H86 2015
 618.9289´1656–dc23   2014022740

ISBN: 978-1-138-01696-5 (hbk)
ISBN: 978-1-138-01697-2 (pbk)
ISBN: 978-1-315-74747-7 (ebk)

Typeset in Sabon
by HWA Text and Data Management, London

The eye of man hath not heard, the ear of man hath not seen, man's hand is not able to taste, his tongue to conceive nor his heart to report what my dream was.

William Shakespeare

Amazing really that something as tiny as the self should contain contending subselves and that these subselves should themselves be constructed of subselves and on and on and on.

Philip Roth, *Operation Shylock*

Contents

Photos

Foreword

As the academic term comes to a close, I find myself looking back over the last two years with a sense of marvel over what has happened in both my professional and personal life as a result of my association with Kelly Hunter. I could not have predicted that our collaboration would provide me the opportunity to build a program at my university focused on the Hunter Heartbeat Method. Our alliance has begun a transformative journey for all involved – my students, my colleagues across campus who are combining artistic implementation with empirical science, resulting in visionary research between disciplines, educators in the local public and private school systems, and most importantly, the children and families affected by autism spectrum disorder (ASD).

As a faculty member in the Department of Theatre at The Ohio State University, I serve as the Director of a three-year, longitudinal research study, entitled 'Shakespeare and Autism', which engages the question of whether drama – particularly Shakespeare – can break through the communicative blocks of autism and whether a creative modality such as the Hunter Heartbeat Method, can produce long-term benefits for children with ASD. The Hunter Heartbeat Method (HHM), created by UK actress and director Kelly Hunter, and described in the chapters that follow in this invaluable guide, is undergoing scientific study. The research project represents an innovative partnership between the arts and sciences, specifically between The Department of Theatre at The Ohio State University and the Nisonger Center, a University Center for Excellence in Developmental Disabilities. While I lead a team of theatre students and faculty in the implementation of the HHM in the schools, a research team from the Nisonger Center is guiding the empirical research. This project grew out of a previously established relationship between The Ohio State University and the Royal Shakespeare Company.

What distinguishes and differentiates Kelly's work is that she has made deep connections between Shakespeare's themes, rhythmic language and storytelling and linked them to the specific communicative challenges faced by those with ASD. The games that comprise the Hunter Heartbeat Method purposefully target specific areas of communicative challenge for those on the spectrum and employ Shakespeare's plays as the vehicle through which communication can be made more accessible and enjoyable. The research team is assessing the ability of these games to affect significant and long-term change to the core features of autism.

Before I describe the research study that evolved from Kelly's pioneering work, let me acquaint the reader with how I was introduced to the Hunter Heartbeat Method. Just a few months before meeting Kelly Hunter, I had the opportunity to see her riveting portrayal of Hermione in The Royal Shakespeare Company's production of *A Winter's Tale*, in Stratford-upon-Avon. Given that the lasting impression of Kelly was as the larger-than-life Hermione, I found her down-to-earth demeanor and frankness refreshing.

Only an hour after meeting her, I found myself playing characters from *A Midsummer Night's Dream* with a group of children with autism between the ages of three and seven. This was my first experience working with children with autism and I admit to having been somewhat apprehensive about my ability to give them what they needed, a concern that has been echoed by the first-time teaching artists who implement the work. Yet, within moments of our start, with the resolve and compassion resonant of Hermione, Kelly enveloped child and adult into the magical world of Shakespeare's *Midsummer*. I noticed that I began to feel empowered and encouraged which I would later discover were key components of the Hunter Heartbeat Method. Shortly after joining that introductory session with Kelly and the children, she approached me to direct the research project. My response was immediate – I wanted to be a part of this new and dynamic approach to working with and connecting to children on the spectrum.

As the reader will learn in Kelly's description in the chapters that follow, The Hunter Heartbeat Method transforms the complexities of Shakespeare's poetry and storytelling into a sequence of games that are specifically tailored to meet the needs of children with ASD. The work employs the rhythm of the iambic pentameter and the exploration of movement, emotional and vocal expression of Shakespeare's characters. Although the games are fairly easy to learn, the scope and breadth of their impact are influenced by subtle nuances in implementation and in skills that develop and grow with time, repetition and practice. Kelly modeled these nuances in her leadership and although others will make this work their own, describing some of the quality and stlye of her facilitation will provide insight for aspiring teachers.

I observed Kelly's loving and maternal presence with each child during that introductory first session. She had never met these children and yet she dove in without hesitation and began to nurture them as if each were her own. Kelly made adjustments as needed to meet the individual needs of the children which highlighted the adaptability of the work as well as the need to discern how each child may specifically benefit. Some children needed to be held closely while others worked better from a distance; some needed a bit more time to hear about 'the why' of each game, while others needed to just play with no explanation. Her loving embrace of each child coupled with command of the space figured prominently in her execution of the method.

Simply put, when running the games that comprise The Hunter Heartbeat Method, 110 percent of the focus needs to be on the children and that focus needs to be infused with compassion and intention. A typical session is an hour maximum and that hour requires total and concentrated focus. More specifically, all children and especially children with autism have varied degrees of verbal, movement, social and communicative abilities. Therefore, the practice requires that the instructor adjust the games to specifically address each child's ability to achieve the game's intended target(s) whether they are eye contact, spatial awareness, emotional expression, motor skills, or language skills. Responding to the energy and comfort levels of the children is equally important. This degree of attention makes it possible to adjust to their individual needs with compassion (e.g. patience for the reluctant child) and intention (adjusting the instruction to meet the child's level of implementation).

In addition, the same degree of intention and compassion must be applied to oneself. In other words, the work and the children will shape the experience of the teacher as much, if not more, than the reverse; it is imperative that the teacher give her/himself the time and space to learn from each child and the changing impact of each game. The work is always in process and the connections forged between teacher and child will change and grow. The work requires a level of openness and willingness to be vulnerable with the children, playful expression, and an ability to adjust to varying needs and unpredictable moments of expression. This work requires compassion, curiosity and patience with the children and with oneself.

Kelly leads by responding to the child's entire experience as opposed to fixating on one aspect or even the target of a particular game. In other words, there is no point in focusing solely on the objectives for the games if the children are not feeling empowered and enjoying the work, which is why there is such a strong emphasis on play. Every game that comprises the Hunter Heartbeat Method joyfully empowers the children. However, joy manifests itself differently with each child and the level of engagement from each child may vary. It is the instructor's responsibility to make engagement possible for the children. For example, if a child seems to find participation particularly distressing, adapting to allow him or her to watch and observe is perfectly acceptable. It is a compassionate teaching artist who will recognize that the child is experiencing distress rather than interpreting his or her behavior as disruptive or resistant.

Although most of the children are comfortable sitting in the circle to begin, many children on the spectrum find transitions very challenging. The transition from their previous activity and space to the new activity and space may come with a set of coping mechanisms which can vary from child to child. For example, some children may tug and pull at the threads on their socks, while others fixate on or pick at the skin on their fingers. Other children may respond by running around to try to alleviate the tension and others state their displeasure at being involved in the activity. Recognizing the behavior as a symptom of transition distress will relieve an instructor from feeling responsible for having caused the behavior and will enable her/him to focus on easing the transition. Employing trial and error methods for easing their transitional distress, as opposed to trying to enforce a necessary halt to their behavior, increases the likelihood that the children will feel that their distress is acknowledged and being taken seriously. What follows tend to be less distressing transitions which in turn begin to minimize the need for coping mechanisms. This compassionate perspective has informed and impacted all the areas of my teaching making me a more intentional and humanistic listener and has helped me to see and understand a child's struggle before I jump to an errant conclusion or assumption that it represents purposeful opposition or intentional disruption.

Another of Kelly's leadership strengths is an attitude and expectation that the children will be perfectly capable of doing whatever she asks of them. She makes it possible for the children to move beyond the scope of their experience, to try something new and in some cases that something is merely to witness the game that is being played in the circle. Kelly enters each session with the expectation that the children will follow her lead. Her instructions are delivered with brisk confidence coupled with a tone of loving invitation which leaves little time or desire for the children to resist. Kelly literally leans forward when facilitating the work and I have found that this small adjustment makes for more engaged, energized and assertive facilitation.

Kelly's expectation that all will be well sets up the dynamic that everyone will follow as a matter of course and that everything is attainable; what a beautiful way to approach the world. In some cases helping a child tap out the heartbeat rhythm by placing a hand over theirs and guiding them to their heart may be the help they need but there is no rush; there is merely attention to what it appears the child needs and an expectation that they can accomplish anything.

It has been a privilege to lead the Hunter Heartbeat Method in the U.S. and to contribute to this innovative body of research at The Ohio State University which adds yet another dimension to Kelly's work. Following the requisite university protocols for research projects, our study was initiated by first establishing and coordinating relationships with the district, state and local school administrators. The partnerships with the public city schools made it possible to begin the pilot. As the research team identified the parameters for the scientific study, I prepared a team of actors for the pilot and our first group of children who were between the ages of 8–14.

The pilot project consisted of twelve weekly hour-long sessions with two groups of eight middle-school children. The workshop sessions took place outside of the routine of the daily curriculum; several parents expressed their gratitude that an afterschool program was being offered for their child, which hadn't previously been an option for them.

The pilot project provided the research team with the necessary data to continue on with the full-length study. The Nisonger Center's research team is assessing the HHM and specifically its efficacy in producing a positive impact on adaptive functioning skills including social and communicative skills, pragmatic language and facial emotion recognition. General measures of overall satisfaction with the program are also part of the research and evaluation.

To date, a total of 54 students have been involved in the research. The full-length research project began with hour-long workshops that were held during the regular school day once a week for a total of 42 weeks. This group of children was matched with a comparison or 'control group' of children, who were placed on a waitlist and both groups received pre-tests administered by the research team. Each group was tested midway through the project and the preliminary results were very promising. Those children who participated in the workshops showed measured improvement in social functioning, overall adaptive functioning, and language skills and showed greater improvement than the children in the waitlist-control group.

The Hunter Heartbeat Method has taken root at The Ohio State University and is expanding outward. An innovative model for interdisciplinary research between the arts and sciences has been established. While our initial university commitment was to implement the HHM in order to serve the research needs, I quickly realized that we could extend the reach of Kelly's groundbreaking work by training university students from several disciplines. I developed an interdisciplinary 'Shakespeare and Autism' course which provides training in the Hunter Heartbeat Method and will be offered independent of the research study.

Both the research and university course enable teaching artists comprised of faculty, graduate and undergraduate students the opportunity to learn and guide the HHM while engaging in long-term community building with children on the spectrum. They obtain practice and experience in the live 'laboratory' setting of a classroom working with children from public city, public suburban and private schools within our major metropolitan area of the United States.

In the United States, The Centers for Disease Control estimate that one in sixty-eight children were identified with ASD during the most recent U.S. census in 2010 and that the incidence of ASD is expected to grow nationally and globally. Professionals in the arts and science communities are establishing major connections as we work together to apply Kelly's methodology to this growing segment of the population with ASD. The work brings children on the spectrum together with artists to share a safe space of creation and transformation; ultimately it is changing the lives of all of those involved. While the results of the Shakespeare and autism research are not conclusive at the time of this writing, the preliminary findings suggest that Kelly's work is making significant impact on the communicative processes and social skills of children on the spectrum. Furthermore, the groundwork has been set for ongoing Hunter Heartbeat workshops and teams of teaching artists are being trained who can research and implement the work in their classes, theatres, communities and in their personal lives.

The work has provided meaningful learning and life experiences for all involved. Over the last two years I have received countless emails and comments from parents and aides expressing the impact of the work on their children. One parent said, 'The repetition and modeling that your program offers while focusing on emotions and imagination, has a lot of potential and really seems like something that can help my daughter.' Another parent shared that her son had joined their local drama club and that his participation in the HHM sessions had provided the bridge that enabled him to take that step. Another mother who came to observe one of our sessions said that she had never seen this playful side of her son. She had been wondering what was changing his previously withdrawn and shy demeanor at church into one that was outgoing and animated and after watching him take part in a workshop she felt confident that his participation in our weekly sessions was the reason for this change in him.

As it turns out, the children have had far more to teach us than we could have ever imagined. For example, one of the children reminded me that once a decision is made to fully commit to a choice, to act on anything, that action can never be undone. This child appeared to be momentarily paralyzed with terror at the thought of making the wrong choice and yet despite that terror, he, and every child like him, entered the playing space and fully committed to the imagined emotional and physical life of Caliban, Prospero, Ariel, etc. And every child followed this with an expression of satisfaction and pride at realizing a hidden talent, an ability to imagine and then bring these creatures to life through the body and spirit. I am reminded that we all need to dive into the unknown and emerge feeling proud of our bravery and ability as educators, artists, parents, aides, and caregivers; we are all equal players in this endeavor.

I have tremendous appreciation for those children who work arduously every day to overcome the overwhelming anxiety that just existing in this world can sometimes present, and then to release themselves into an hour of human connection and purposeful play. I am reminded again and again that navigating the world can take tremendous effort and that we all need to be a bit more compassionate for those whose terrain has more rocks. Other children share what I can only categorize as the epitome of innocent and unadulterated joy after throwing a surprised face around the circle or crying out with fear as Trinculo the jester from *The Tempest* discovers a strange beast with 'four legs and two voices!' Their joy is immeasurable and contagious.

If there is one thing that all of these children possess and that I wish more people possessed, it is the gift of authenticity. The world would be a much better place, if it had even a tenth of the authentic straight-shooting delivery that these children have shared with us. I am honored to have been given the opportunity to share these precious hours whether in the early morning or the late afternoon, where we have shared a safe space to bare our playful souls with each other. I do not remember a time when I experienced such pure child-like joy as a teacher; every week our souls were filled to the brim with the innocence and bravery of these remarkable children. These seemingly fleeting moments of beauty as the children taught Caliban his name or gave Prospero cramps, while playing the games of *The Tempest*, will remain with all of us for a lifetime.

I am forever grateful to the teams of actors who have poured their hearts and souls into this work and to all of the families, teachers, administrators, collaborative research partners who agreed to join us, and most importantly, to all the children who have been there to create this magical journey with us. I cannot thank Kelly Hunter enough for entrusting me with her work which allowed me to share it with these amazing children; we have been able to forge connections through the imagination, language, and spirit of Shakespeare. This work has made me a better teacher, actor, director, and most certainly a better human being.

Collaborations wherein empirical scientific research is able to quantify the impact of the arts and specifically the impact for those with ASD are few. The timeliness of *Shakespeare's Heartbeat*, which documents the games that comprise the Hunter Heartbeat Method, has far reaching implications for this burgeoning field of research. The project at Ohio State has evolved into wide-ranging and long-term community partnerships between university and school communities. University students involved in implementing this work have been able to practically apply their craft as part of a groundbreaking research project, which will have deep impact to this ever-growing segment of the population. The work fulfills an increasing need to provide safe and creative space where the growing number of people diagnosed with ASD can explore and develop their communicative skills as well as be empowered to embrace their presence and make their mark on society. The 'stage has been set' for the continued development of this work as it reaches a wider audience and the detailed practice of the Hunter Heartbeat Method provided in following pages will make it possible for the work to reach significant numbers of people living with and impacted by ASD.

After spending the last two years immersed in the world of the Hunter Heartbeat Method, I am eager for others to discover the work, make it their own as well as expand on the research, which has only just begun. The Hunter Heartbeat Method represents the vision and inspiration of an actor, teacher and humanitarian and I'm happy to say, my friend and colleague. It is a visionary methodology and resource for teachers, artists, parents, aides and all who are interested in transforming the lives of those affected by autism spectrum disorder.

Robin Post
Ohio State University

Acknowledgements

This book is dedicated to children at The Glebe School, Bromley 2003–2006: Martin, Lizzie, Joseph, Nicola, Jack, Matthew R., Joe, Perry, Matthew C., Francis and Chelsea. Children at The Village School, 2009–present day: Brandon, Will, Junior, Holly, Ayat, Sarah, Allen, Christopher, Farah, Nabil, Joseph, James, Abdi, Monica, Kevin, Mustapha, Shanelle, Leon, Tyrek, Fraz, Zane, Sharona, Ali, Ilyas, Ronak, Andy, Zaynab, Muno, Charlotte, Halima, Kirsty, Dhilan, Nasir, Mahin, Fuad, Jenny, Harus, Lucas, James and Iman. Children from the New York Armory Project, 2011: Clarence, Cynthia, Zyree, Mahleik and Anthony. Children from the Shakespeare and autism research project in Ohio, 2011–2014: Ashvini, Nathaniel, Audrey, Aleah, Joey, Luke B., Luke W., Mary, Meredith, Nathan, Robert, Sarah, Wesley, Ben, Devin, Haley, Jaret, Michael, Julian, Neil, Dashay, Zach, Adam, Chris, Connor, Jayce, Sam, Bethany, Zach, August, Nick, Rayvon and Trey. Children from Welcombe Hills School, Stratford upon Avon, 2010–present day: Hattie, Scott, Ian, Matthew F., Ben, Christian, Julian and Misty.

Thanks to:

- Claire Sainsbury.
- Karin Wilson, Heather Avigdor and the staff of St Mary's and St Peter's Primary School.
- Chris Crawley, Chris Collins and the original Touchstone Shakespeare Theatre team, Joe England, Matt Sutton, Liz Hurran and Victoria Duarri who, together with James Rayment, Mel Woodbridge and Laura Hayes, collaborated to create so many of these games.
- Jurina Krafkicova and Karen Calamaro, without whom this work would never have progressed over the last five years.

- Greg Hicks, Katy Stephens, Sam Troughton, James Gale, Hannah Young, Samantha Young, Kirsty Woodward and Gruffudd Glyn, who took just one week in 2010 to show me the transformative power of this work.
- Will Dagger, Harrison Unger and Drew Lewis, who worked with me at the Armory in New York City.
- The Shakespeare and autism research team in Columbus, Ohio, led by Robin Post with Kevin McClatchy, Genevieve Simon, Andrew Trimmer, Jirye Lee, Alex Boyles and Mahmoud Osman, whose dedication, talent and humour over the last three years have taken these games to a whole new level.
- Jacqui O'Hanlon, RSC.
- Marc Tassé, Maggie Mehling and Lesley Ferris at Ohio State University.
- The Ohio State University Department of Theatre MFA Acting class of 2014.
- Michael Dobson, whose encouragement has been invaluable.
- Bessa at Café Toscana and Mrs Pepperpot, who helped me when I wrote this all down.
- My family, Albert, Charlie and Tom.
- Harriet Affleck at Routledge, John Hodgson and Holly Knapp at HWA, and Dave Cradduck.

My heartfelt thanks to Talia Rodgers, whose encouragement and vision have made this book possible.

Introduction

These drama games are sensory, physical and fun to play. They are created to heighten the children's awareness of themselves and provide an opportunity to explore emotions, which may otherwise be overlooked. Making eye contact, improving spatial awareness, developing facial expressiveness and building language skills are key targets within the games as well as introducing imaginative play and the notion of playing a part. Shakespeare is used not for educational means, but rather to wake the children up to their own lives, directly challenging their disassociation of mind and body. The vast majority of children, no matter where they are on the autism spectrum, can access the games.

The first time I gave a Shakespeare workshop was in a men's prison in Darlington in the northeast of England. I was performing in a small-scale tour for the RSC in 1991 and I'd volunteered to run a session for prisoners based on *Measure for Measure*. I prepared arduously, reading and re-reading the play, dividing speeches and photocopying scripts. Once inside, I handed these scripts to the assembled group of thirty men, who looked at the pieces of paper and then looked back at me staring blankly with what appeared to be shame. Not one of them could read.

It never occurred to me not to continue. Without hesitation, I abandoned the scripts and with them my many hours of preparation. Since looking at the words wasn't an option, it seemed obvious that I should speak Shakespeare's language and they could learn it from me, which is after all the way humans first learn to talk – somebody teaches them.

I used short phrases from the play concentrating on themes of mortality; I knew the scenes backwards so I didn't need to look at the words. I encouraged the men up on their feet and improvised a body-sculpting game, using still body images as starting points and then bringing the characters to life by prompting the lines for them to speak. This way they learnt the language quickly and helped each other remember the phrases – had we had the time, we could have done the whole play.

Inspired by the play, a heated debate quickly ensued around the question of the transience of life. In less than two hours the group had transformed from thirty men ashamed at their lack of literary skills to a collection of individuals with fierce and passionate opinions on the big life questions. Our time was up too soon and I felt that I had barely scratched the surface of the potential in the room, theirs and mine. Inevitably I never saw these men again. However, my improvised non-scripted Shakespeare workshop that afternoon was to become the foundation for my future method of teaching.

Ten years later when I ran Touchstone Shakespeare Theatre my motivation was not to introduce Shakespeare to children in order that they become well-behaved theatre go-ers, but rather to invigorate their souls at that particular moment in their lives, right then and there in the room. I had read a beautiful book by the American poet Louis Zukofsky – *Bottom: On Shakespeare* – published in 1963 when he was in his late forties and I was just born. The book is a piece of scholarship and a work of art: a poet's response to the human resonance of Shakespeare's language, and my inspiration for creating this work.

Zukofsky makes a vibrant case for understanding Shakespeare's poetry as an obsessive exploration of the definition of love. To this he devotes a long chapter, which begins with a 'conversation' with his son:

Son: What do you drive at or derive where you've jotted
           down *Def.* in the margins of fourteen hundred and
           ten pages, double column, of your complete plays and
           poems of William Shakespeare? Def equals deaf?
I: *Def* equals definition
Son: Whose?
I: Shakespeare's – of love.
Son: Yes?
I: It speaks and sings of a proportion: *love is to reason as the eyes are to the mind.*

Love is to reason as the eyes are to the mind! In one phrase Zukofsky encapsulates Shakespeare's definition of love as seeming to have clarity whilst at the same time presenting itself as utterly baffling. He continues with an analysis of each play, giving page after page of examples showing how Shakespeare uses four keywords – eyes, mind, reason and love with a particular emphasis on eyes – in an endless variety of poetic forms to create his sensory definitions of seeing, thinking and loving.

In *A Midsummer Night's Dream*, he achieves the heart of his theme with Bottom:

> ... and yet, to say the truth, reason and love keep little company together nowadays

and with Bottom again, as Pyramus:

> I see a voice

And talking to his own eyes

> Eyes do you see? How can this be?
> Oh dainty duck, oh dear.

Not only through the character of Bottom but equally so with Helena

> Love looks not with the eyes but with the mind.

And Hermia

> Methinks I see things with parted eye,
> Where everything seems double

In *King Lear* the mad king meets the blind Gloucester on the heath

Lear: What, art mad? A man may see how this world goes with no eyes. Look with thine ears...
No eyes in your head? Your eyes are in a heavy case... yet you see how this world goes.

Gloucester: I see it feelingly

In *Hamlet*, two keywords come together

> My father, methinks I see my Father...
> In my mind's eye, Horatio

Whilst the two remaining keywords are joined by Imogen in *Cymbeline*

> Love's reason's without reason

And elsewhere for Helena in *All's Well that End's Well*

> What power is it that mounts my love so high
> That makes me see, but cannot feed mine eye

For Prospero as he watches Miranda and Ferdinand fall in love

> At the first sight they have chang'd eyes

And speaking to Miranda as she remembers her past

> But how is it
> That this lives in thy mind? What see'st thou else
> In the dark backward and abysm of time?

And Duncan in *Macbeth*, (expressing a struggle so common to autism)

> There's no art to find the mind's construction in the
> face

Shakespeare's definitions are a poetic exploration of how it *feels* to be alive, how it feels to expressively communicate. This is a fundamental concept of his writing and was my jumping off point for inventing this work.

By focusing on Shakespeare's definitions of seeing, thinking and loving, I stumbled upon the processes that those on the spectrum find so difficult to achieve. Children with autism experience varying degrees of difficulty with communication, all of which can be understood as a disassociation of body and mind. Expressing feelings, making eye contact, accessing their mind's eye and their dreams, keeping a steady heartbeat and recognizing faces are all part of the autism dilemma and all are poetically explored by Shakespeare. Embedding these unattainable skills within games derived from moments of Shakespeare, which the children could play and thereby benefit from, seemed like the most natural thing in the world and formed the basis for these games.

The Heartbeat Circle, which begins and ends every session – everyone sitting together, hands on hearts and beating out the rhythm of a heartbeat whilst saying 'Hello' and practising facial expressiveness – is inspired by the intrinsic power of the iambic rhythm, the second fundamental concept which underpins this work. Shakespeare's language, his definition of love, explores how it *feels* to be alive whilst he uses the rhythm of the heartbeat to reveal the ever-changing specificity of those feelings; the rhythm is the *life* of the feeling.

The heartbeat is also one of the first sounds we hear in the womb, and arguably offers a sensation of safety and warmth for all human beings including those with autism. I make Heartbeat Circles with non-verbal children, using the iambic to give space and time for 'internal panics' to soothe; the positive effects for some of these children seem to reach far beyond the classroom.

One such child is Robert, paper-thin and hard to reach, who does anything to stay behind his wall of gibberish song rather than speak. His teacher works tirelessly with him, gently demanding day-by-day that he use language to communicate with her. Supported by my weekly workshops he has made progress, the significance of which struck home early in 2011 when he broke his arm, after which his teacher wrote this note:

Dear Kelly,
This morning we went to visit the Pony centre where we usually horse ride, they had an open day and our children took part in a competition. They all did brilliantly, but unfortunately right at the end when the horses were lined up, the lorry scared the horse, he moved and Robert fell off. He was a bit upset and was pointing to his elbow so I decided to take him for a check up to hospital. According to his mum, Robert hates hospitals and she always struggles badly with him once they enter. I was waiting with him in the waiting room. He was distressed, upset and crying a little bit.

After few minutes he took my hand, placed it onto his heart and started saying 'He-llo, He-llo', exactly as we to do it with Kelly in drama. After about three minutes he changed 'Hello' to 'Good-bye' and then he stopped. He calmed himself down completely and stopped crying. He kept singing his songs (as he always does) and asked me to hold his elbow. It was amazing to see how he calmed himself down and that he thought about this. I was pleasantly surprised, so I have to share it with you!

February 2011.

Jurina Krafcikova, Robert's teacher.

It doesn't always go well. Sylvia, a non-verbal seven-year-old girl prone to screaming came to one of the Heartbeat Circles I had set up for non-verbal children. She sat on my lap, holding my hand against her heart and beating the rhythm out on her chest. After a while she fell asleep, during which I continued the heartbeats and when she woke up a few minutes later she resumed her connection with me, joining in with the rhythm. She spent the whole session in this way, rocking between sleep and drowsiness, whilst I kept the heartbeats going. Her teachers were amazed, they'd never seen her so relaxed.

'It's the rhythm of the heartbeat, it has incredible power' I said with pride, venturing to tell people how effective my work was becoming and looking forward to seeing Sylvia again. In she came for the next session, sat herself down on my lap, and we began exactly as we had the previous week. After a couple of minutes I felt a burning sensation in my forearm that wasn't going away. In the time it took me to look down I realized that Sylvia was biting me, hard like a baby shark as if in protest to the heartbeat rhythm so opposed to her own inner pulse at that moment. She wasn't letting go and it really hurt. We prised her jaw from my body, the pain numbed by the sting to my pride and a lesson truly learnt; the interior rhythms of a child with autism are changeable, unknowable and precarious.

I worked with her many times after that day, she never bit me again and I continued to learn about autism listening with my whole soul to her rhythms. Every time a non-verbal child sits on my lap or by my side during these circles I continue to learn how to be sensitive to their needs, attempting to read the thoughts and feelings that they can't articulate for themselves. Little by little, with weekly repetition these children become familiar with the Heartbeat Circle, increasingly allowing it to soothe them.

The soothing power of the iambic rhythm together with Shakespeare's poetic exploration of how it feels to be alive make up the two fundamental concepts which underpin the games in this book. Together these games form the methodology known as The Hunter Heartbeat Method.

Playing the games/Using the book

All the games are played within a large circle marked out on the floor, around which the children and adults sit together, side by side. No scripts are ever used: nothing but your bodies and voices are needed. The games are physically engaging and most have a few lines of Shakespeare embedded within them, which you teach the children through prompting. It is essential for you to have learnt the words before playing with the children.

The games are comprised of three stages: demonstrating, playing and sharing. First, the actors demonstrate the game inside the circle and the children watch. Next, everyone gets up on their feet and the actors pair up with the children, spreading around the room to play in pairs or small groups. Finally, everyone returns to the circle and each pair or small group share their game for the rest to watch.

For each game in the book I give a brief introduction, outlining the characters and narrative involved and identifying the specific traits of autism, which the game addresses. I follow this with how to demonstrate the game, including any text that should be learnt. I then offer guidance for playing with the children whilst helping them overcome their difficulties.

I set out the games as they were originally created, with actors demonstrating, children and actors playing together and myself as the leader of the sessions. Ideally, the children play one to one or two to one with actors, whilst a leader facilitates the workshop – but it is also possible to lead and play with the children alone. Working on your own you demonstrate the games by yourself or choose the most able child to demonstrate with you, inviting the children to play with you inside the circle thus sharing the game at the same time. You can use picture cards as teaching aids, comprising a single word, expression or character name, together with an appropriate picture.

Shakespeare's plays are packed with moments of transcendence and these are embodied within the games as 'points of ecstasy' (POEs), moments where effort culminates in achievement and it's

Photo 1 The circle works for a small group (photo © Jirye Lee)

clear that the game has been accomplished. The expression POE is found throughout the book and serves as a reminder that the games must be pleasurable; the children's communicative progress is dependent on sharing a sense of playfulness with the adult. Whether you are actor, teacher, parent or leader it is essential to let the children know that you have come to play with them and that above all, the games will be fun.

A certain amount of trial and error is inevitable when you initially play these games; the scope of difficulties is so wide across the spectrum that not every game or strategy will prove beneficial for every child. The games are not theoretical ideas; rather they are tried and tested techniques invented by playing with children, creating games around their individual personalities and unique traits of autism. Ensure that you take your time to discover the children's specific needs, experimenting with your approach until you find something that begins to challenge the child's particular communicative difficulty. Each game can be modified to suit any child no matter where they are on the spectrum.

The book is divided into two parts, games of *A Midsummer Night's Dream* and games of *The Tempest*; it's possible to introduce the children to the games using either play.[1] The guidance and advice

---

1   Extracts follow the Folger Shakespeare Library edition, available online at www.folgerdigitaltexts.org. Texts for the games are sometimes paraphrased or simplified for the children.

Photo 2 The circle also works for a larger showing of the games (photo © Nick Spratling)

for playing with the children in Part I establishes a foundation of practical knowledge, which is further developed in Part II. The final chapter of the book is a short resource for playing with the children highlighting the key skills accumulated throughout the games.

The games of *A Midsummer Night's Dream* were created with a group of children between twelve and fifteen years old, whom I played with over a concentrated period of two years at the Glebe School in Bromley, London. These were the first games I made, using Shakespeare's poetic exploration of eyes and love to combat the children's autism. The games constitute the fundamental beginnings of the work and can be played with all children no matter where they are on the spectrum.

The games of *The Tempest* have been developed over eight years and form the basis of the Shakespeare and Autism Research Project in Ohio. Whereas the games of *A Midsummer Night's Dream* explore Shakespeare's themes of seeing and loving, *The Tempest* games focus also on themes of liberty and imprisonment using the characters of Caliban and Ariel to provide a deeper means for the children to express themselves.

Some of *The Tempest* games use the same framework as those of *A Midsummer Night's Dream*, whilst others are new. All the games hold on to the essential aim of the work – using the fundamental themes of Shakespeare to combat the communicative blocks of autism. Whichever play you choose to start with, I recommend introducing the games to the children in the order they are set out in the book, allowing Shakespeare's narrative to unfold whilst the games become more challenging.

Before you start, here are the practical ground rules for playing:

- Mark out a circle on the floor, big enough for everyone to sit around. Make a small cross in the centre so that the children know where the middle is.
- A maximum of ten children is ideal with as many supporting actors/teachers as possible.
- A session should last approximately an hour. Try to set aside the same hour daily or weekly to play with the children.
- Always begin a session with the Hello Heartbeat Circle followed by 'Throwing a face', using a facial expression of your choice. Then play one or two games, which you have prepared and that you think will specifically benefit the children.
- Take time for the children to absorb and practice, there is no need to introduce a new game every week; the games are short, fun and repeatable and it is in their weekly repetition that progress can be made.
- Leave a couple of minutes at the end of each session for the Goodbye Heartbeat Circle.

Part I

A Midsummer Night's Dream

Love looks not with the eyes but with the mind
(*A Midsummer Night's Dream*, I, i, 240)

Chapter 1

Games to begin

Games

- The Heartbeat Circle
- Throwing the face

The Heartbeat Circle

Begin every session with a Heartbeat Circle. This gives the children an opportunity to transform their faces and voices within a safe environment, allowing them to experience brief moments of acting from the very beginning of the workshop. The repetition involved in the game offers invaluable practice for the children to observe and explore different facial expressions for themselves. The game is based upon the rhythm of the heartbeat taken from the iambic pentameter, which underpins Shakespeare's verse, and is shown to have a calming, almost meditative, effect on the children. The game is simultaneously demonstrated, played and shared at the same time.

Demonstration/playing with the children

Sitting around the circle, everyone places their hands on their hearts and slowly beats out the rhythm of a heartbeat together, creating a collective pulsing sound as a group. Once this rhythm has been established, start to say and repeat the word 'Hello' using the heartbeat rhythm to naturally underpin the words: 'Hel-*lo*, Hel-*lo*, Hel-*lo*.' Everyone in the circle joins in and the atmosphere is easy and enjoyable. Try to make eye contact with everyone in the group and during these initial minutes take the opportunity to learn about the children. How are they today? How difficult is it for them to

Photo 3 Making Heartbeats (photo © Jirye Lee)

keep the rhythm? Are they willing to speak? Can they make eye contact? Are they relaxed and comfortable?

After about a minute say 'Now rest your hands' and place your hands in front of you on the floor encouraging the children to do the same. Suggest to the group that you give yourselves a 'round of applause', by clapping your hands in the shape of a circle in front of you, making a 'round'. Cup your hands when clapping as this makes a duller sound and is easier on the ear. This small routine of finishing a game with a quiet round of applause creates a boundary from which the children understand the game has ended and can be used after each game or exercise.

Now establish the rhythm with the collective heartbeat again, but this time take turns to say 'Hello' one person at a time, starting with yourself and continuing around the circle, everyone keeping the heartbeat rhythm alive using their hands on their hearts. If after encouragement a child doesn't want to join in, they can pass. Once the round has returned to you finish the turn with 'Now rest your hands' and once more suggest a round of applause.

Next choose a particular facial expression, selecting initially between happy, sad or angry. You can say for example 'let's make an angry face' and encourage everyone to try. Never ask the children to feel angry, just ask them to make an angry face. Actors are often asked to imagine something that brings on a particular feeling whether it is something from their own life or something they conjure up that will make them feel sad, happy, angry, etc. This is not the direction you want to take with the children, rather you want them to understand what an emotion looks like and for them to try to replicate the outward picture. Begin by demonstrating with your own face so that they may try to mirror what you provide. It is very possible that the children begin to feel the emotion they are showing, but the fundamental point is not to begin with the inner feeling but rather to start with the outer facial expression.

Now start the 'Hello' circle again and during this next round of 'Hellos' encourage everyone to keep the chosen expression in their face and voice whilst making the heartbeat rhythm, saying 'Hello' one by one around the circle. The 'Hello' should sound and feel completely different now that it has an expressive feeling behind it. Initially for some of the children there will be no difference at all. This is another opportunity to learn what the children are capable of in terms of understanding facial expressions and creating them. Make several rounds of 'Hellos' practising different expressions.

Finally offer the children the chance to 'take a circle'. One child sits on the cross in the middle and chooses an expression for the whole group, for example happy. You then encourage everyone to assume a happy expression. Remember, don't ask them to feel happy, simply to make the face. Establish the rhythm once again, making sure that there is a steady pulsing wall of sound, creating a safe environment within which to play. The child in the middle proceeds to say 'Hello' to everyone in turn around the circle, maintaining the happy face and voice. Each person says 'Hello' in return, also keeping the happy face and voice, giving everyone the chance to make their particular 'Happy Hello'.

Once the child in the middle has exchanged 'Hellos' with everybody, rest your hands and then give a warm round of applause. Repeat this exercise so that each child has had a chance to take a circle. It may be slow work but it is time well spent. After the three initial faces – happy, sad and angry – have been established you can add three more: fearful, surprised and disgusted. Additional faces can be added at any time, which introduce and illuminate the predominant features of a character. 'Mischievous' is an excellent face with which to introduce Puck whilst 'lovestruck' is a useful face for the characters in *A Midsummer Night's Dream* who have had their eyes 'tricked'. Both mischievous and lovestruck are popular

Photo 4 Making angry heartbeats (photo © Jirye Lee)

choices with the children and you can introduce them early on to support the first games in the book. Once every child has taken a circle, the group is ready to play 'Throwing the face'.

At the end of each session spend the last few minutes making a 'Good-bye Heartbeat Circle' by swapping 'Hellos' for 'Goodbyes'. Keep this as a group activity, there is no need or time for each child to take a circle. Choose a calming expression with which to say goodbye, the idea is to send the children back to the outside world with increased tranquility and confidence – a final round of 'angry goodbyes' wouldn't seem quite right. As before with the 'Hellos', take this opportunity to make eye contact with the group and use these last few minutes to see how the children are. There is usually a marked difference between the 'Hellos' at the beginning and the 'Goodbyes' at the end, when the children have relaxed during the session, found their voices and are more willing to be playful.

Heartbeat Circle for non-verbal children

You can adapt the Heartbeat Circle for non-verbal children and those with very low cognition. At best it offers a calming womblike experience, which becomes almost meditative and can last up to twenty minutes. The children's anxiety can be potentially soothed by the predictable prospect of each steady beat that is offered in the rhythm. Encourage willing parents, teachers and actors to join the children and sit around the circle, one child per accompanying adult if possible.

Demonstration/playing with the children

Everyone who can places their hands on their hearts and slowly beats out the rhythm of a heartbeat together. Once the rhythm is established, the adults begin to say 'Hello', exactly as you do with the regular Heartbeat Circle. The idea is for the children to join you in the rhythm and to begin to make sound if possible; they will need encouragement, guidance and praise.

If the children can't physically make the heartbeat by themselves, guide their hand to their heart and beat out the rhythm together. Get comfortable with the child and continue making the heartbeat with them; a close physical relationship is essential and your confidence with the child is key. Some children are immediately at ease with the heartbeats whilst others feel happier having the rhythm made on their backs. Playing with a child for the first time I say something along the lines of 'I'm going to make contact with you using my hand, is that ok?' If they are very unhappy being touched then choose handclaps to make the rhythm. Experiment until you find what the child will physically tolerate during the session. An adult or capable child can take a circle in the centre, saying hello to the children in turn.

Photo 5 Saying 'Hello' (photo © Jirye Lee)

Allow the child's internal rhythm to be absorbed into yours whilst you keep the heartbeat going; listen as deeply as you can to their inner life, feeling when they can join you in the heartbeat and when they need to shake or rock to their own interior time. Initially they may remain predominantly inside their own world and only 'join you' for one or two heartbeats in the space of 20 minutes but with patience and repetition the child may connect with the heartbeat a little more each session.

If the child moves away from you, but stays in the room do not immediately run after them – the last thing you want is to be chasing a child. Continue the heartbeats and offer your other hand out to the child to show them you would like them to join you again. This often works and you may find that the child needs to move away several times but ultimately returns. If you decide to go to the child to encourage them to return to the circle ensure that the other adults continue the heartbeats without you; it is essential that the wall of comforting sound is not broken.

You can pass a hand mirror around the circle as the heartbeats continue, allowing each child to examine their own reflection when the mirror comes to them. Encourage them to make eye contact with their own image, repeating the 'Hellos' as they look; it may be that this is the first time they have had the opportunity to slowly

Photo 6 Using the mirror (photo © Tom Wright)

explore their own face. For the last few minutes you should change from saying 'Hello' to saying 'Goodbye', creating a short Goodbye Heartbeat Circle with which to end.

For some children the twenty-minute Heartbeat Circle may initially represent the full extent of their drama activity. If practised daily or weekly over a prolonged period there may be marked progress in terms of their eye contact, rhythmic communication and in some cases joining the adults to begin to make sound. Guidance and advice for playing all the games with children at the low end of the spectrum is found throughout the book.

Throwing the face

This game is played immediately after the Hello Heartbeats with everyone still sitting around the circle. It is an excellent warm up for acting, providing the children with a transformative challenge, without demanding that they stand up and 'act'.

The game introduces two characters from *A Midsummer Night's Dream*; Puck, a mischievous spirit, and Bottom the weaver who is taking a walk in a forest. During a pivotal moment in the play Puck plays a trick on Bottom, turning his head into that of a donkey. Initially that is all you need to know in order to play. The drama of the game brings Puck's trick to life whilst allowing the children to continue exploring the plasticity of their faces, having begun with the 'Heartbeat Hellos'. This is serious work for the children, whose facial muscles may rarely move, yet it must appear to be nothing more than fun.

Throwing the face is a key game and appears throughout the book in various forms. Once you have established its framework, replace the donkey face with key facial expressions using happy, sad and angry to begin with and progressing to surprised. fearful and disgusted. It can be helpful to choose an expression that corresponds directly with the games you have selected for your session. I highly recommend using surprised as a facial expression to throw around the room.

Demonstration

Two actors sitting on opposite sides of the circle play Puck and Bottom; they raise their hands, one saying 'I'm Puck' and the other 'I'm Bottom'. Puck assumes the face of a donkey, with buckteeth, hands making ears, twitchy nose and making an 'EE-AW' sound.

Photo 7 Throwing a happy face (photo © Jirye Lee)

Photo 8 Catching a happy face (photo © Jirye Lee)

The face should be playful and very much alive. Puck is going to 'throw' the face to Bottom on the count of three and Bottom should be ready to 'catch' the face straight away.

Slowly say '1, 2, 3 throw' at the end of which Puck 'throws' his face toward Bottom. The action from Puck should be as if a mask is being flung from his face, requiring some physical and vocal effort. Bottom immediately assumes the donkey face with an element of surprise as if it has landed from nowhere, his hands making ears, nose twitching, buckteeth and making the EE-AW sound. He keeps the face until you instruct him to throw it again.

Now choose another actor or child to be the 'catcher' and instruct Bottom to get ready to 'throw the face'. When both players are ready to 'throw' and 'catch' use the instruction of '1, 2, 3 throw'. In this way the face can be 'thrown' and 'caught' around the circle to actors and children until everyone has had a turn and you ask for it to be thrown to you. Vary the choice of catchers using pairs and small groups. By the end of the round Bottom's donkey face, or indeed whichever face you have thrown around the circle, should be embedded in the children's sense memory. To finish the game, throw the face to the whole group so that everyone 'catches' it together for a final time. Finally ask the group to drop the face, rest their hands and give a round of applause.

If you are demonstrating alone, you can use picture cards to introduce the characters. Make the face of the donkey yourself and 'throw' it to the most able child in the circle. From there, slowly teach and play the game, using yourself as the thrower and the catcher as often as you need.

Playing with the children

Play as a group in the circle for this game. Ensure that all the actors commit totally to making the donkey face (or whichever facial expression you have chosen to use) in order that the children fully understand the game and want to make the face themselves. Commitment is vital as in everything you do with the children; seeing an adult commit to the playful creation of a donkey face allows the children to feel secure within the lightheartedness of the workshop. They will then be much more likely to play with you and try the games themselves.

Some children will need a lot of physical encouragement in order to make any change to their expressions. As the face is thrown around the circle, the actors sitting nearest or on either side of a child should help them as much as they need; catching the face at the same time and encouraging the child to begin to make the transformation by copying. It's important to leave this encouragement to the actors who are sitting nearest; calling out or demonstrating from across the circle could be overwhelming for the child.

The use of acting and transformation is key: your encouragement should always be active, demonstrating the donkey and allowing the child to copy and join you, as opposed to telling them to do it whilst you remain inactive. This ground rule goes for all the games, take the initiative to play and act in order for the children to join you and never allow the children to feel they are doing anything other than playing.

Once the Heartbeat Hellos have been made and faces have been 'thrown' and caught around the circle, the group will be ready to be on their feet and play some games.

Chapter 2

Fairyland

Reason and love keep little company together, nowadays.
(*A Midsummer Night's Dream*, III, i, 145–6)

Titania, queen of the fairies, is tricked into falling in love with Nick Bottom, a weaver whose head has been transformed into a donkey by Puck, a mischievous spirit. The games of Fairyland use the story's visual comedy to allow the children immediate access to acting, introducing fundamental targets of the games: making eye contact, improving spatial awareness, encouraging facial expressiveness and improving speech and language.

The initial games concentrate solely on the body progressing through to games that use vocal sounds and finally introducing language. The guidance in this chapter is key, introducing the idea that you discover what the children can't do for themselves and begin to show them how to achieve it.

The games

- Four 'Shadow' games
- I'll follow you
- Sounds and shadows
- Lovestruck
- Puck's trance

The characters

- Puck
- Titania
- Bottom

The targets

- Making eye contact
- Improving facial expressiveness
- Improving spatial awareness
- Improving speech and language skills

Four 'Shadow' games

The 'Shadow' games are classic games of 'he's behind you' adapted to challenge the children's difficulties whilst bringing the story of Puck and Bottom to life. The physical playing style is slightly exaggerated; Bottom's fear and Puck's mischievousness can be heightened and playfully explored.

The 'Shadow' game

Puck is following Bottom through the forest; he is unseen, a shadow. For the purposes of the game the circle becomes the forest and may be described as such to the children. Initially Bottom is unaware he is being followed and then he becomes increasingly fearful as he senses the presence of Puck before he turns round to find him.

The game encourages physical co-ordination and increased spatial awareness. The short moment of eye contact at the end of each game marks the first chance for the children to explore their partner's eyes. No physical contact is made when playing the shadow games, the 'catching' is achieved with eye contact.

Demonstration

Two players stand together in the circle. They introduce themselves as Bottom and Puck. Puck stands directly behind Bottom, an arm's distance away. Bottom slowly starts to move around the circle and Puck follows him, copying everything he is doing with as much precision as possible, whilst maintaining an arm's distance behind – the perfect shadow. Bottom is as physically expressive as possible, hopping, skipping, dancing, stretching, bending and leaning in different directions. He varies the speed in which he moves around the circle but, crucially, he never runs.

After a minute or two Bottom senses that there is someone behind him and begins to try to find Puck, at which point the game gains momentum as Puck tries not to get caught, creating the classic game of 'he's behind you'. Bottom becomes increasingly 'fearful' as he realizes Puck is behind him and Puck becomes increasingly 'mischievous'. When Bottom feels the time is up, he whips round to find Puck and both players make a few seconds of eye contact at which point there is a natural intake of breath creating the game's Point of Ecstasy. This is a good moment for a round of applause from the group. The players then take a breathing space before they swap parts and play again.

Playing with the children

The 'Shadow' game should always be fun; encourage the children to enjoy the playfulness of hiding behind another person whilst trying not to get caught and the culmination of eye contact at the end of every turn, which creates the Point of Ecstasy.

Your ultimate aim no matter where the children are on the spectrum is for them to experience what a game *feels* like. No child with autism is the same, what may be challenging for one will prove almost too easy for another. Some will need full support to begin with, they may have no concept where 'behind' is and require your complete physical assistance. To begin playing the game with children at the lower end of the spectrum, place their hands on your shoulders and lead them around the room, encouraging them to copy simple rhythmic movements. After three or four steps in one direction, turn around and make a concerted effort to find the child's eyes. Although the game calls for the moment of eye contact to be a 'snap' of surprise, this may be too alarming for the child. Read their body language as attentively as you can, assessing how gentle you may need to be to introduce the challenge of looking into each other's eyes.

In reverse place your hands on their shoulders and gently encourage them to move forward in simple rhythmic steps as you stay behind, copying them clearly and demonstratively, and then gently turning them round to face you and find your eyes. Ensure that you keep your instructions short, clear and friendly, rather than speaking in long sentences, which will prove overwhelming whilst they are attempting to achieve a new physical activity. Keep the turns short and controlled, giving praise if and when eye contact is made. Use this first time up on your feet with the child to learn about their strengths and weaknesses whilst showing them that the games are fun to play and share. As you play the game with the child over weeks and months encourage them to become increasingly independent as the movements become part of their physical sense memory.

For children at the higher end of the spectrum the game's simplicity provides an opportunity for them to make imaginative choices whilst challenging their own spatial awareness and eye contact. These children may ostensibly find this game easy although there will very likely be something in the game which they find challenging. Play with them slowly and carefully, reading their bodies and eyes until you find where they may need help. Encourage them to play with dexterity and humour taking the initiative as much as they can. Picking an imaginary apple from a tree and biting into it whilst walking around the circle/forest is useful for Bottom to mime and is perfect as a starting point for copying. Ensure that the children begin to develop greater self-control of their bodies through playing the game, stretching the physical possibilities of shadowing. Finally make sure that they achieve longer periods of eye contact at the end of each turn.

When you have repeated the game a few times come back to the circle to share with the whole group.

The 'Shadow' game with invisible Puck

In this next version Puck has become invisible and freezes like a statue when Bottom turns round to find him. Bottom turns round three times to try to catch Puck but only catches him out the third time.

Demonstration

Begin as before with two actors in the circle playing Puck and Bottom. Puck follows Bottom around the circle at an arm's length behind him copying all his movements. Only this time Puck is invisible. The first time Bottom turns round, Puck freezes like a statue in whatever position he is in. Bottom stares into Puck's eyes for a few seconds, Puck doesn't move a muscle. Bottom becomes confused and decides to carry on walking through the forest. As soon as he turns away to continue walking around the circle, Puck unfreezes and returns to following him as his shadow. No moment should ever be rushed.

Bottom then turns round to catch Puck a second time and they repeat the same 'freezing' action. Increasingly confused, Bottom turns away again and on his third and final attempt, he turns round very fast and catches him before Puck has the chance to freeze. They both make true eye contact providing the POE. After a breathing space the partners swap roles and play again.

Playing with the children

The same tips for playing the first 'Shadow' game are applicable here, depending on the abilities of the children. The moment of looking into 'invisible eyes' should be explored fully, especially with those who have the cognitive ability to understand the concept of invisibility. With some of these children the fact that Puck is invisible seems to eliminate their fear of eye contact, as if being unseen renders the eyes unseeing, allowing the child to explore looking into another's eyes and to experience being looked at without fear.

When you have repeated the game a few times, return to the circle to share with the whole group.

The 'Shadow' game with playful Puck

In this version Puck wildly exaggerates all Bottom's movements, whilst still shadowing him and avoiding being caught. This game requires a higher level of imaginative play and should be played by the children once they have experienced and mastered the first two games.

Demonstration

Two actors stand in the circle and begin as before with Puck an arm's length behind Bottom ready to shadow him. The rhythm of the game remains the same; Bottom walks around the circle being shadowed by Puck and he tries to 'catch' Puck three times. Puck freezes for the first two and is caught at the third creating the POE. In this version it is the shadowing itself which is different; Puck now exaggerates the movements of Bottom, picking up on a tiny gesture or movement or sensation and creating a bigger version of it. A small step from Bottom becomes a big stamp from Puck. A little skip from Bottom becomes a leap in the air from Puck. A confused sigh from Bottom becomes a weeping wail from Puck. This released exaggeration creates a heightened moment of humour each time Puck has to freeze.

Playing with the children

This one change in the game may prove very challenging for some of the children. The key is to keep the exaggerations precise; it is still a game of shadowing. The phrase 'copying but more' is useful.

For children who seem fearful of making the exaggerations you can play a 'More or less' game. On your instruction of *'more'*, Puck makes his exaggerated shadow copying. On the instruction of *'less'*, the shadowing becomes tiny. It's fun to make tiny copying movements, like a little mouse, and then burst into exaggerated movements, like a giant, on a one-word instruction.

Some children will feel released by this version and may need to be reminded that it is still a game of copying and that Puck doesn't want to get caught. The dramatic tension of the game lies in the contrast between Puck's naughty spirit, which is teasing Bottom, and the situation of the game in which he is trying not to get caught.

When you have repeated the game a few times, return to the circle to share with the whole group.

The 'Shadow' game with dancing Puck

In this final version Puck dances like a wild fairy. His mischievous life force has been released and although ostensibly he is still Bottom's shadow, his physicality reveals his true spirit.

Demonstration

Two actors stand in the circle and begin as before with Puck an arm's length behind Bottom ready to shadow him. The rhythm of the game remains the same, Bottom walks around the circle being shadowed by Puck and he tries to 'catch' Puck three times. Puck freezes for the first two and is caught at the third creating the POE. It's important that Puck still follows Bottom around the circle and remains behind him at all times trying not to be seen. However, instead of any attempt to copy or exaggerate Bottom's movements, Puck now dances like a silent wild fairy, skipping, hopping and grooving to his heart's content, keeping Bottom in his vision at all times, so that he can freeze as soon as Bottom turns around. As always, the partners take a breathing space before swapping roles and playing again. The abandon and joy with which this dancing is demonstrated is vital if the children are to emulate it.

Playing with the children

The children may require no encouragement in the game at all – some of the most unlikely children I have worked with start to dance with surprising candour. But it is more likely that you will find yourself demonstrating some sort of dance for them to copy. If this is the case then keep it simple. The dancing does not have to be expansive or indeed last very long, it may simply be a rhythmic movement of hand, foot or face. It is very useful for the child to hook onto a repetitive rhythm.

When you have repeated the game a few times, return to the circle to share with the whole group.

I'll follow you

As Puck follows Bottom through the forest he boasts that he can transform himself into different creatures and elements. The sounds of the game, a horse, a hound, a hog, a headless bear and a flame of fire are derived from Puck's language as he shadows Bottom deeper into the forest.

'I'll follow you' invites the children to use sound without words, directly challenging the children's vocal flatness. In the first stage of the game they listen to Puck's poem and when they hear each name and noise they make matching sounds challenging their voices beyond their normal use. In the second stage they physically create body shapes, which bring the creatures to life. The game allows the children to engage physically and vocally with Shakespeare's language whilst experiencing a small act of transformation.

The first stage

Demonstration/playing with the children

Before you play, memorize these lines:

Puck: I'll follow you, I'll lead you about a round
    Sometime a *horse* I'll be, sometime a *hound*

A *hog*, a headless *bear*, sometime a *fire*,
And *neigh*, and *bark*, and *grunt* and *roar* and *burn*
Like *horse*, *hound*, *hog*, *bear*, *fire* at every turn.

Everyone sits around the circle. Begin by saying that Puck can transform into different animals and elements and that together you're going to make the sounds that Puck makes. Speak the poem slowly, stopping after each name or noise to make the accompanying sound, beginning with the neigh for the horse and continuing through to the end.

The poem will sound like this: (sounds in capitals)

I'll follow you, I'll lead you about a round
Sometime a horse I'll be,
NAYAYAYAYAY

Sometime a hound,
WOH WOH WOH WOH WOH

A hog,
SNORT SNORT

a headless bear,
ROOOOAAAAAR

sometime a fire,
ZAZAZAZAZAZAZAZAZAZAZAZA
And neigh,
NAYAYAYAYAY
and bark,
WOH WOH WOH WOH WOH
and grunt
SNORT SNORT
and roar
ROOOOAAAAAR
and burn
ZAZAZAZAZAZAZAZAZAZAZAZA

Like horse,
NAYAYAYAYAY
hound,

WOH WOH WOH WOH WOH
hog,
SNORT SNORT
bear,
ROOOOAAAAAR
fire at every turn.
ZAZAZAZAZAZAZAZAZAZAZAZA

The NAYAYAYAYAY is high and soft

The WOH WOH WOH WOH WOH is low and threatening

The SNORT SNORT is a made breathing in and up through the nose

The ROOOOAAAAAR is loud and deep

The ZAZAZAZAZAZAZAZAZAZAZAZA is quiet and exciting, like crackling firewood.

The actors join in with the sounds straight away. If you're playing alone, you can use picture cards to support you. The poem gathers momentum and speed with the final line giving the quickest pattern of changes. The ultimate noise of burning fire produces a release of energy providing the POE.

Some children may join in with the sounds straight away during the demonstration, which is great and should be praised. Stay seated around the circle and speak the poem again, encouraging the children to join you and the actors.

The more variety you find in your voice the better they will exercise theirs through copying you, encouraging them to stretch their vocal capacity. These five sounds offer a vocal range, high to low and loud to soft, providing exercise for their voices. For the children, this is a game of bringing Puck's transformative powers to life in order to tease Bottom, but at the same time it allows them to begin to explore the sounds they are capable of making, potentially unlocking their voices.

Many children will naturally add movement to the sounds straight away and they may well know their own signs for the animals. These are not to be discouraged, but it's important to remember that all that is required for this first stage is to explore the sound.

The second stage

Still sitting around the circle, repeat the poem again, encouraging the children to add physical life to their sounds with their arms and upper bodies. A shake of the head for the horse, hands and arms into paws for the hound, a fist to the nose for the hog, a big, raised arm movement for the roar of the headless bear, and crackling fingers for the fire. Encourage children who are already making their own movements to be more expansive. Make sure that the physical life does not diminish their vocalization, but rather adds to it.

The third stage

Everyone stands up on their feet around the circle, and repeats the exercise for a final time. Encourage the children to use their whole bodies to make the transformations allowing time and space to fully explore the experience.

Sounds and shadows

The games so far have explored one scene in the play; Puck following Bottom through the forest. To bring the scene to life with sound and physicality 'I'll follow you' is played as a 'Shadow' game and completed by 'Throwing the face' providing the opportunity for the children to embody Puck's transformations whilst he shadows Bottom, culminating in throwing Bottom the donkey's head. The 'Shadow' game with dancing Puck is the one to use. It's not as complicated as it may sound.

Demonstration

Two actors stand in the circle, Puck standing an arm's length behind Bottom ready to play. As Bottom begins to move, Puck shadows him but this time he transforms himself into the shape of the first creature – the horse. When he is ready, Puck neighs:

NAYAYAYAYAY.

At which point Bottom turns round and Puck freezes. He is invisible. Bottom looks at invisible Puck and after a few seconds he returns to walking around the circle, increasingly fearful and confused. Puck returns to shadowing him, this time assuming the shape of the hound. When he is ready Puck barks:

WOH WOH WOH WOH WHO.

At which point Bottom turns round and Puck freezes. He is invisible. Bottom looks at invisible Puck and after a few seconds he returns to walking around the circle, increasingly fearful and confused. Puck returns to shadowing him, this time assuming the shape of the hog. When he is ready, Puck snorts:

SNORT SNORT.

At which point Bottom turns round once again and Puck freezes. He is invisible. Bottom looks at invisible Puck and after a few seconds he returns to walking around the circle, increasingly fearful and confused. Puck returns to shadowing him, this time assuming the shape of the headless bear. When he is ready, Puck roars:

ROOOOAAAAAR.

At which point Bottom turns round and Puck freezes. He is invisible. Bottom looks at invisible Puck and after a few seconds he returns to walking around the circle, increasingly fearful and confused. Puck returns to shadowing him, this time assuming the shape of the fire. When he is ready, Puck sizzles and crackles:

ZAZAZAZAZAZAZAZAZAZAZAZA.

Now Puck assumes the donkey face and 'throws' it to Bottom, who 'catches' it. This creates a very good POE for the end of the sequence.

In another version narrate the poem from your place in the circle while the actors demonstrate, with Puck making the sounds when he hears the cue words.

Playing with the children

The combination of the two major games may prove initially challenging, the fundamental hurdle being the addition of sound. All the 'Shadow' games so far have been played in silence with Bottom in control of the games' rhythm, deciding when to turn around to catch Puck. Now the opposite is true as Bottom turns round because he hears Puck, thereby giving Puck control of the rhythm of the game.

The addition of sound also has the effect of heightening both players' sensory awareness, especially that of Bottom. You can help the children accordingly, reminding the child to listen out for the sound of the animal and encouraging Puck to move around in silence before he makes his next noise. The tension and drama of the game is to be found in the silences between Puck's sounds. This is the first of the *listening silences,* which are developed throughout this book.

Encourage the children to increase the intensity of their emotions each time Bottom turns around; Puck's mischievousness and Bottom's confusion create a humorous drama and the throw of the donkey head at the end of the game is a culmination of this comedy, creating the POE for both players. When you have played the game at least twice through, allowing the child to play both parts, come back to the circle to share with the whole group.

Lovestruck

This is a game of eye contact built around the moment that Titania, queen of the fairies, falls in love with Bottom. The sleeping Titania has had magic juice squeezed into her eyes, whereby on waking she will fall in love with the first creature that she sees. That creature is, of course, Bottom with his donkey's head. Her 'tricked eyes' provide the comedic drama of the game; she stares lovingly into the eyes of the donkey unable to pull her gaze away, until overcome with embarrassment, he finally turns his eyes away from her.

The fundamental aim of this game is for the children to explore making eye contact. The 'Shadow' game will have given you the chance to encourage the children to look into your eyes, but whereas the 'Shadow' game chiefly focuses on spatial awareness with a short burst of eye contact at the end, this game demands that eye contact is made and sustained for a long period. The eyes themselves are the essential focus of the game.

This full sequence between Titania and Bottom is played in four stages. By the time you have explored each stage with the children you will have learnt many of the key components of this work. The first stage introduces eye contact and the second stage adds facial expressiveness and physical movement. In the third stage, with the addition of language, you will begin to prompt words to the children and experience Shakespeare's connection between words and feeling leading to an understanding of 'instructive playfulness'.

The final stage permits increased physical freedom, allowing the scene to come to life.

Although it may be that some children find the initial stages easy, do explore each stage with them as you will learn where their strengths and weaknesses lie, giving you both the opportunity to make progress. No physical contact is made between the two players, the 'catching' is all in the eyes.

The Doyoyoying!

The 'Doyoyoying!' is a humorous device used to capture the moment of Titania's 'tricked eyes' making eye contact with Bottom. You may decide to split into pairs around the room to practise, but I prefer to use it as a group activity.

Demonstration

With everyone sitting around the circle one actor introduces herself as Titania and proceeds to make the 'Doyoyoying!' If you are teaching alone, simply demonstrate by yourself.

Think cartoon, specifically a cartoon character whose eyes widen and leap out on stalks when falling in love at first sight. Join your

Photo 9 The Doyoyoying! (photo © Jirye Lee)

thumbs and forefingers together creating two circles; place them to your eyes making 'spectacles' touching your own face. Now stare through the circles and, cartoon style, as if your eyes are bouncing out on stalks exclaim the sound 'Doyoyoying!' while at the same time shaking your 'finger spectacles' a few inches away from your face.

Practise this with the children. You can create a simple practice rhythm for the whole group saying '1, 2, 3 Doyoyoying'. Do this three times then rest your hands before having another go. You can also take turns around the circle, one person at a time taking a turn to make the 'Doyoyoying!' Additionally you can use 'Throwing the face', but in this case 'Throw the doyoyoying!'

LOVESTRUCK

Two actors stand in the circle, facing each other an arm's length away, but not making eye contact. One is Bottom with his donkey head. All through the game he keeps his hands as ears and uses the donkey face as expressively as possible. The other player is Titania, wide-eyed and loving.

THE 'DOYOYOYING' SEQUENCE

To begin the sequence, Titania looks into Bottom's eyes, they make eye contact and breathe in, he with fear and her with delight:

Next, she makes the 'Doyoyoying!'

Next, maintaining eye contact, Titania says 'I love thee'

Next, Bottom says 'EE-AW' with embarrassment and moves one step sideways avoiding her eyes.

Thus ends the sequence.

To begin again, Titania takes one step toward Bottom, 'catches' his eyes and they begin the sequence once more.

They repeat the sequence four times. On the fourth and final time, Bottom does not say 'EE-AW' but joins in unison with Titania for the 'Doyoyoying!'

Next, they say 'I love thee' in unison creating the POE.

With each repetition of the sequence Titania's affection and Bottom's embarrassment become increasingly heightened leading to an escalation of emotion and comedy as they head toward the POE.

Playing with the children

The 'Doyoyoying!' tackles what for many of the children is a crippling problem: making and sustaining eye contact. Ensure that the game is as playful and funny as possible, countering the child's intense struggle with an equal measure of play and enjoyment. Focus first on the comedy of the embarrassed donkey alongside the doting expression of Titania as expressed through her lovestruck eyes. Let the children enjoy your acting and encourage them to invent their own versions of the two characters so that the moment of making eye contact is as easy and natural as possible; allow them to find your eyes through play.

In this simple almost stationary version, with just one sidestep between the two players, you have the chance to develop a rhythmic pattern to the game, which the children may enjoy and hook onto. Establish a pronounced sidestep with a strong simple rhythm so that it becomes organic to the child and use this rhythm as a 'safety net' in which to explore the facial expressions and the eye contact more easily. Alternatively you can omit the sidestep altogether and play a completely stationary version of the game.

Focus on the facial expressions of the wide-eyed queen and the embarrassed donkey as a close up version of the scene, as if a camera were filming both your faces as intimately as possible. With each game the child plays encourage them to discover further plasticity of the face, yours and theirs, within which eye contact is a central activity. Take your time to adjust to the child's tempo, it's a new physical language they are learning; be patient and loving and never ever give up on their capacity to play.

When you have repeated the game and the children have swapped parts come back to the circle to share with the whole group.

Adding words

The third stage adds a beginning to the game, giving the characters an activity; Bottom is singing to keep fear at bay and Titania is waking from her sleep. This short prologue offers the chance for the children to enjoy a moment of transformative acting before the game of eye contact begins. It also offers the chance to begin prompting.

You have no scripts for these games and the children will hear and learn the words through you. Echolalia, the automatic repetition of sound made by another person, is a common trait of autism and most children will repeat Shakespeare's words back to you when they hear them. This can seem encouraging although it's often difficult to know whether the children comprehend the meaning of the words or if they are just repeating them. In light of this your prompting must always engage with feeling and facial expression, encouraging the child to do the same.

Your role as prompter is key, you are offering the child the stimulus to speak; however you are not simply asking them to repeat words back to you parrot fashion, but rather you are using emotion and expressiveness, which lie embedded within Shakespeare's language, to simultaneously bring words and feelings to life. Encouraging the child to copy you should inspire the child to connect sensations and emotions to the act of speaking. Ensure that your prompting is alive with feeling, a sharing of a character's emotion through words. This single line of Titania's has an intense poetic charge rooted within it whilst the comedy comes from the fact that she is speaking to a donkey.

Demonstration

Before the workshop memorize this line:

Titania: What angel wakes me from my flowery bed?

As before, two actors stand in the circle, facing each other an arm's length away. One is Titania with her eyes closed; she is sleeping. The other is Bottom with his donkey head; alive and playful.

To begin Bottom starts to hum or sing to himself. The tune of 'Happy birthday', with words or without, works well. (You don't need to use Shakespeare's words here; the fundamental key to this moment is that Bottom's singing embodies the sound and physicality of the donkey. Add in some 'EE-AW's if you wish. That is all.)

As Bottom sings, Titania begins to wake up, clearly being woken by the sound of Bottom's voice but not yet looking at him. Yawning and stretching, she speaks her words:

What angel wakes me from my flowery bed?

Bottom stops singing and Titania turns her face and eyes to see Bottom for the first time.

Photo 10 'What angel wakes me from my flowery bed?' (photo © Tom Wright)

The two players perform one 'Doyoyoying!' sequence as before:
Titania looks into Bottom's eyes, they make eye contact and breathe in, he with fear and she with delight:
Next, she makes the 'Doyoyoying!'
Next, maintaining eye contact , Titania says 'I love thee'
Next, Bottom says 'EE-AW' with embarrassment and moves one step sideways avoiding her eyes.
They continue as in the previous game; making four rounds, finishing as before by making the 'Doyoyoying!' and saying 'I love thee' in unison.

Playing with the children

Before you take on either of the roles, spend some time teaching the children Titania's line by prompting; speak the words with expressive emotion and repeat the line a few times, thereby stimulating the child to copy you. If the child is very new to these games, try saying 'Copy me' every time before you speak the line. Make sure they can see your face as you prompt the words. Many children will memorize Titania's words on first hearing. Other children may always require prompting no matter how many times you play the game – adapt your prompting to complement their difficulties.

If a child struggles with language prompt them with one or two words at a time and look directly at them so they can copy your facial movements. Encourage them to use expressiveness in their voices and not just to repeat the words. Use yourself as their model to copy, show them, don't tell them. You often need less instruction than you think in order to play and the instruction you use should be clear and precise. Their learning comes through copying you and attempting to play with you.

I sometimes use signing as another strategy to bring the words to life. This line of Titania's has a particular physical beauty in it if using sign language. The 'angel' is made with your two hands crossed in the shape of a butterfly moving and quivering upwards in front of your heart. The hands burst apart on the word 'wake', the 'flowery' sign is a fluttering of the fingers in front of your nose and finally the 'bed' is made with your two hands resting on the side of your face.

For children who memorize the line easily, your role is more supportive than instructional and you should move away from the front of their faces, taking a position to the side of their head so that the prompting is sound-based and not visual. This sound-based prompting must not lose its expressiveness. Make sure that every time they say the line they are engaging with their feelings as much as possible and don't be afraid to jump back in so they can see your face to remind them of their expressiveness. Children who memorize the lines quickly are likely to repeat them faster at the expense of expression, so your initial prompt should be fully expressed. Your work as prompter is potentially never done.

Once you have introduced Titania's line through prompting you can begin to act the scene and play the game, which will involve you playing one or other part; therefore you may be prompting the child as they play Titania whilst you are simultaneously playing Bottom. The ability to concurrently instruct the children whilst playing your part is fundamental to your success and enjoyment with the children. I call it 'instructive playfulness'.

When playing with the children you must be 100 per cent committed to acting your part, whether you are the lovestruck Titania, Bottom with the donkey head, or any of the characters throughout the book. At the same time stay alive to the fact that the child may need your help and stay ready – whilst playing – to give instruction and lead the children toward their communicative progress. Your aim is to help the child overcome their difficulties whilst you continue playing and acting, gently instructing them if they need prompting with the line or help with any number of issues, physical and expressive, at any one time. With this in place the experience of playing with the children remains absorbing and creative for both of you. This technique is at the heart of the work – without it the games may seem impossible.

When you have repeated the game several times and the child has played both parts, come back to the circle to share with the whole group.

Adding movement

The children are now given a wider physical rein within the game, bringing the scene to life. Instead of being limited to taking one step sideways, both Bottom and Titania move freely inside the circle. This single change has a transformative effect, making it harder for Titania to 'catch' Bottom's eyes, and easier for Bottom to 'hide' his eyes. This increased physical challenge creates an intensified dynamic to the drama and further releases the game's comedic potential.

Demonstration

Two actors are in the circle, Titania, who rests asleep on the floor and Bottom who stands anywhere he chooses in the circle. This version begins with Bottom singing or humming to the tune of 'Happy birthday'. As in the previous game the key to this moment is that Bottom's singing embodies the sound and physicality of the donkey. He believes he is alone in the forest and sings to 'show he is not afraid'. In this version there can be added bravado to his voice, bordering on the ridiculous; adding 'EE-AW's to the singing or humming greatly enhances the effect.

As she hears Bottom's voice, Titania slowly awakes and stands up from the floor, not yet seeing Bottom. She speaks her line:

What angel wakes me from my flowery bed?

Next, wide-eyed, she moves closer to Bottom and standing an arm's length away from him, she finds his eyes and the two players perform one 'Doyoyoying!' sequence:

Titania looks into Bottom's eyes, they make eye contact and breathe in, he with fear, she with delight:

Next, she makes the 'Doyoyoying!'

Next, maintaining eye contact, Titania says 'I love thee'

Next, Bottom says 'EE-AW' with embarrassment and this time instead of taking one sidestep away he now moves around the circle, removing his eyes from the gaze of Titania and trying to get away from her. He must not run. He repeats 'EE-AW' a few times expressing his confusion, shyness and embarrassment. Titania follows him, wide-eyed and lovestruck, moving in front of him to try to 'catch' his eyes.

Titania moves around the circle in any way she chooses, trying to 'catch' Bottom's eyes. As soon as she catches them, she holds eye contact once more and they perform another 'Doyoyoying!' sequence. Everything is the same as the previous game other than the two players move freely around the circle. When they have finished and after a little breathing space, the actors swap roles and play again.

Playing with the children

It's vital that free rein does not result in chaotic running about. Running, in any of the games, is a dead end and all you can do is get hold of the child, stop them running and start the game again. There is no communicative drama to be found in the child running around the room. If you have a 'runner' (by that I mean a child who is compelled to run around the circle as fast as they can) or a keen 'spinner' or a compulsive 'falling downer' my strong advice is to hold on to them physically and with patient demonstration show them how you and they are going to play the game. This is not at the expense of any of your lightheartedness, but it is very much part of your instructive playfulness; the instruction being we do not run, but we can still play. Be gentle and firm; remember that the child may never have been told this before, or even if they have, they weren't told by you.

If it's clear that your child has a physical instinct of 'flight' then play this final stage in a different way; do not let them move freely around the circle. Keep the sidestep as the main physical movement in the game but enhance it with two or three additional steps so there is still a new dynamic to be discovered. This version, free from running, will be controllable, allowing you to explore eye contact, facial expressiveness and language.

The challenge is to make your acting more attractive to the child than her running. Bottom *must* take his eyes away from Titania's gaze because he is so alarmed and embarrassed; meanwhile Titania *must* gaze into his eyes because she is lovestruck. Show them the 'feeling' of the movement, encouraging them to copy. If and when you sense that the child has begun to explore the acting and is unlikely to run away, allow her free rein for a few seconds at a time; be patient with yourself and her, running is likely to be a long-term habit, hard to break quickly.

For those children not compelled to 'flight' you will by now have played the game many times, concentrating on various deconstructed elements. You will know the children's communicative strengths and weaknesses, therefore use this final version to support them where they need help and allow them to build on their self-esteem where they excel.

Ultimately this game focuses on the exploration of making eye contact; seeing into another human's eyes and allowing yourself to be seen. Each time you make eye contact with the child consider it a gift; it is not an inconsequential moment. Even if you have had to crawl around on your hands and knees to find their eyes, and even if it is only a glimpse that you have caught, that moment is a shared endeavour well worth the effort.

When you have repeated the game a few times, return to the circle to share with the whole group.

Puck's trance

This game offers an alternative approach for Puck to cast his spell over Bottom. The first stage is played in silence and the second stage adds words. If you are building a narrative by creating a sequence of games, this game provides an ideal bridge between 'Throwing the face' and 'Lovestruck', showing Puck's pivotal role in the story.

'Puck's trance' is a classic drama game adapted to combat the difficulties of autism; it directly challenges the children's spatial awareness and simultaneously offers further opportunity for focusing the eye. Introduce this game once the children have played the 'Shadow' game as it explores the same moment in the play but provides an opposing physical experience for the children; in this game the players are facing one another. There are several games of trance throughout the book of which this is the simplest and the best one to start with.

The first stage

Demonstration

To begin, two players stand face-to-face in the circle, just an arm's distance apart. One is Puck and the other is Bottom. Puck places the palm of his hand in front of Bottom's face. The distance should be comfortable for both players, ideally one hand span away; any closer is intimidating and any further away lessens the impact of the game. Bottom stares into the palm of Puck's hand as if hypnotized by him. Both players concentrate on keeping an equal distance between eyes and hand for the duration of the game; it is as if Bottom's eyes are transfixed by a magnetic force in the palm of Puck's hand.

Puck slowly begins to move his hand in any direction he chooses, maintaining his palm in the same position to Bottom's face at all times. As Puck moves, Bottom follows the palm of Puck's hand with his eyes, smoothly re-positioning his head and body as much as he needs in order to maintain eye contact with the hand.

Puck's movements slowly grow to encompass his whole body until he begins to move slowly around the circle. As he does so, Bottom follows him as if pulled by the invisible magnetic force, staring at all times into the palm of Puck's hand. Puck has all the power and Bottom has none. If Puck walks backwards, Bottom is seemingly pulled forward and if Puck walks forward, Bottom is pushed hypnotically backwards. The players slowly continue this magic 'push and pull' for a few minutes, and when Puck has had enough he gently makes one handclap, which breaks the 'spell'. At the handclap both players take a breath together and share a moment of eye contact, creating a POE. The players then immediately swap roles. An alternative to the handclap is for Puck gently to blow air on Bottom's forehead as if to wake him from the trance. The demonstration is over when both players have played both parts.

Playing with the children

This game will throw up challenges for nearly all children on the spectrum, testing their spatial awareness to its limits and demanding a focus from their eyes that renders them insecure. If the child struggles intensely with eye contact this game will be tough, it is best played for short spells of concentrated effort at as slow a pace as possible.

Photo 11   Leading the child (photo © Nick Spratling)

Begin by allowing the child to have the power of the game, i.e. they play Puck and their hand hypnotizes you. Encourage them to move as slowly as they can. If they go too fast, you can stop playing, take some breathing space and ask them to begin again. I often say something along the lines of 'your magic won't work unless you play slowly'. Some children may need a lot of initial encouragement, in which case use your instructive playfulness. Suggest directions in which they can travel around the circle and even help them move their hand up and down whilst at the same time remaining hypnotized by that hand! It's a challenge, but it may be the only way they can learn how to play. Above all let them enjoy the potentially new experience of being in charge, reminding them that for these few minutes they have power over you. If the child doesn't clap to swap roles, encourage them to do so, take some breathing space and prepare to take the power of the game.

If the children have no problem staring into the palm of your hand, focus on encouraging them to stretch and extend the physical shapes they make with their bodies and to try as hard as they can to bend their knees while they are moving. Lead them to their own physical extremes so they experience a smooth pushing and pulling – from high to low – stretching on tiptoe to crawling on their bellies,

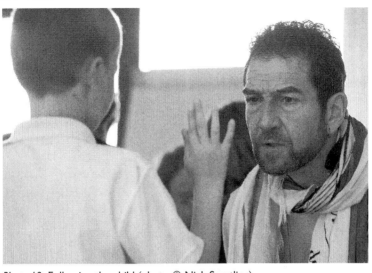

Photo 12 Following the child (photo © Nick Spratling)

never making physical contact with you but feeling connected as if heavy water were pressing between your two bodies.

There will be children who will struggle to connect eye to palm and furthermore it may be hard to describe this new demanding game to those with low cognition. The children will often raise their own palm up to yours as soon as you lift your hand, which results in a rather beautiful dumb show of copying, but doesn't allow the game to progress. If this is the case encourage them to put their hands deep into their pockets, and keep them there.

I have sometimes drawn an eye on the palm of my hand and I've even attached a tiny bell to my fingers to keep the children's attention, both of which have been quite successful. The trouble is that when you take the bell or the drawing away you are back to square one.

My recurring approach is to repeat a single instructive word, 'looking' or 'look' depending on which the child is most familiar with, and at the same time guiding their eyes using my own face, body and soul to direct their gaze to my hand. If and when the child does look to my upheld palm, I give them praise and if their eyes then move accordingly with the small movements of my hand, I offer more praise and stop for a while. Some children may not get beyond this first stage of attempting eye contact with the palm of the hand, and for them this is enough to practise. There is no point walking around the room if the child is not following you.

For children who can follow the hand with their eyes, the ensuing challenge of moving the body in different directions – especially backwards – can be monumental. Some children, no matter where they are on the spectrum, find directional movement almost impossible, resulting in physical awkwardness and leading to constant levels of anxiety. It's important initially to talk these children through the physical demands of the game whilst giving them reassurance. Depending on their cognitive skills you can be as specific as you like, for instance, 'now slowly lift your foot and stretch it back behind you, it's completely safe, good, now place it on the floor and get ready to move the other foot to join it'.

I played this game with a teenage boy in 2011, having played it for many years and with many children. He was a clever, articulate young man but severely challenged by the notion of stepping backwards, let alone trying to do it himself. However he was determined to achieve a backward step, and as he played with me, visibly shaking from head to toe, as if he were placing his feet into a deep black chasm behind him, he let out whimpers of fear and spoke these words painfully slowly, as if they were the last he would utter: 'This ... is ... really ... really *really* ... hard'. With that he achieved the backward step and stood still for a while, breathing in gulps of air, exhausted by his accomplishment.

It's rare to witness the inner thoughts of the children in such a graphic way, and it reminded me that encouragement and praise is essential to the success of the games. For many of the children each game may signify a first-time occurrence and the changes experienced in their bodies can result in feelings of exhaustion and of course elation. It's worth reminding yourself of that every so often.

When you have repeated the game, come back to the circle to share with the whole group.

The second stage

This version adds Puck;s words to the game to bring the scene to life. The words are in fact taken from a later passage in the play when Puck is leading the lovers through the forest, but it works perfectly well here for the purposes of this game.

Demonstration

Before playing memorize these words:

Puck: Up and down, up and down,
    I will lead you up and down
    I am feared in field and town
    Goblin! Lead you up and down.

Play exactly as before, beginning with two players standing face-to-face, just an arm's distance apart. The 'magnetic' quality of the game is the same as before. Puck raises his hand, his palm to Bottom's eyes and as he begins to move his hand, he starts to speak the words, corresponding the 'up and down' of the poem with up and down movements of his hand. As before Bottom follows every movement.

On the word 'Goblin', Puck makes one surprising movement; a little jump with his whole body and assumes the shape of a goblin, hands for horns and mischievous expression. He makes eye contact with Bottom for a split second, creating a tiny POE, then quick as a flash, as though the goblin had never appeared, Puck reinstates the palm of his hand in front of Bottom's face and finishes the last line of the poem, with Bottom following once more. After three rounds of the poem Puck claps his hands, the players breathe in and make eye contact creating a final POE. They take a breathing space and then swap roles.

Playing with the children

Ensure that you have already played the first version with the child so that you can pick up from wherever you left off in terms of their ability; adding the words should be a continuation of playing the game. For some children this version is actually easier, as it has simple directional instructions embedded in the poem. This time you should play Puck first, connecting the up and down instruction in the poem with an up and down movement that stretches both of you as much as possible. You are seeking to find contrast, vocally, physically, and even emotionally, between the worlds of 'up' and 'down'. The words of the poem allow you to cast a 'spell of fear' over the child, which is entirely in keeping with the physical language of the trance. The fun part is breaking the spell by surprising them with the goblin moment, striking a balance between fear and humour and then going straight back into the 'spell' to finish.

When you swap round and the child leads you, use instructive playfulness as much as you need, prompting the lines whilst you are led around the room. When you have repeated the game and the child has played both parts, come back to the circle to share with the whole group.

Chapter 3

Dreams

I'll give thee fairies to attend on thee
And they shall fetch thee jewels from the deep
And sing, while thou on pressed flowers do sleep
(A Midsummer Night's Dream, III, i, 159–161)

Titania leads Bottom deeper into the forest to her flowery bed, where she calls to her four fairies to serve him. Moth, Cobweb, Mustardseed and Peaseblossom appear, bringing purple grapes, green figs and mulberries. Bottom is in the centre of his own dream; a man with a donkey's head attended on by fairies. It is an intense and powerful depiction of a dream world.

A common trait of autism is an adherence to the world of logic; many of the children live by self imposed systems of what they can rationally prove and what they can see. The games in this chapter take the children on a sensory journey introducing them to their own dream world and inviting them to reflect on the existence of their interior lives and their imaginations.

These games take a long time to root themselves in the children's consciousness; for optimum progress the children should play them as part of a weekly routine as they are growing up. I witnessed the depth of the games myself after nearly three years of working with my original group of children in Bromley, London. Having played with them since they were twelve years old, I wanted to see if these fifteen-year-olds could access and explore their own mind's eye images unaided. Within the group was a Romanian boy, he made very little eye contact, was obsessed with bus routes and had minimal verbal skills compounded by English not being his first language. He displayed little empathy and aside from detailing the bus routes of South London he initiated little conversation. He had played with us since the beginning of the project, absorbing the games, exploring Shakespearean stories and developing healthy relationships with the actors and myself.

Cautiously, and with no idea if anything would emerge, I asked the group what they saw in their mind's eye (as opposed to what they saw in their dreams) and without prompting this boy stood up and began to act out the funeral service of his grandmother from his distant childhood in Romania. He acted out characters from his family with physical accuracy, delicacy and emotion, singing snatches of Romanian hymns and totally engrossed in his 'play'. It lasted a good fifteen minutes and everyone was spellbound; it seemed clear that he would never have been able to access this interior world when we had first met him. I have experienced many breakthroughs with children as they become bolder and more confident but this boy's unprompted engagement with his own mind's eye showed me the heart of the endeavour; Shakespeare's soulfulness being used to slowly wake the children up to their own lives.

The games

- The four fairies
- What's your name?
- I have had a dream
- The mind's eye questions

The characters

- Titania
- Bottom
- Moth
- Cobweb
- Mustardseed
- Peaseblossom

The targets

- Making transformations
- Turn taking
- Deepening sensory awareness
- Introducing the mind's eye
- Exploring dreams

The four fairies

The four fairies are called to Titania's bower. This game introduces each one, using simple copying to bring them to life. The fairies have distinctive characteristics, purposefully stretching the children's physical and vocal abilities whilst offering them a transformative challenge. The order in which they are introduced provides the children with a fulfilling, physical experience starting with heavy through to sinewy through to explosive and finishing with peaceful. I confess I have always been surprised how much the children enjoy every aspect of this game, no matter their age, gender or where they are on the spectrum.

Before playing memorize these words

> Moth. Ready.
> Cobweb. Ready.
> Mustardseed. Ready.
> Peaseblossom. Ready.

Demonstration/playing with the children
MOTH

Everyone is standing up around the circle. One actor plays Moth and assumes her starting shape. arms stretched high above her head, hands touching, and feet together, as tall as possible.

The leader plays the voice of Titania and quietly calls Moth's name, making a long vowel sound as if calling for her to arrive from another world.

> Moth.

Moth comes to life; her movements are slow, deep and heavy. Keeping her arms straight and slowly bending her knees, she makes one downward movement with her arms as if they were huge wings closing in slow motion against hot air, gradually pushing them toward her sides. She speaks her name in her deepest, slowest voice possible, making it last as long as she can:

> Mo ... th.

She reaches the end of her name when her arms have reached her sides, hands touching the sides of her legs, knees bent.

She then begins the upward opening beat of her wings, slowly straightening her legs, moving her arms skyward, returning to her overhead position, speaking with a deep unhurried voice:

Ready.

As soon as Moth's demonstration is over, the leader invites the whole group to copy and everyone assumes Moth's starting shape, arms stretched above their heads. When the whole group are ready to play, the leader using Titania's voice, calls Moth's name in the same way as before.

Moth.

The whole group comes to life, replicating the physical movement and voice, repeating the sequence of 'Moth' and 'Ready' three times.
When they have finished the whole group return to standing.

COBWEB

Another actor assumes the starting shape of Cobweb, legs, arms and fingers like a spider's web.
The leader plays the voice of Titania and calls Cobweb's name, making long vowel sounds as if calling into another world.

Cobweb.

Cobweb comes to life, smacking her lips together and moving her arms, hands and fingers as if they were the sticky slow-moving threads of a spider's web. She stands on one leg at a time whilst stretching the other out, all four limbs and fingers engaged in movement. When she speaks her name, she smacks her lips together on the 'b' sounds, repeating it within the name three times.

Co *b...b...b...* We *b...b...b.*

Maintaining the movement she says with verve:

Ready.

As soon as Cobweb's demonstration is over, the leader invites the whole group to copy and everyone assumes Cobweb's starting shape, legs, arms and fingers like a spider's web. When the whole group are ready to play, the leader using Titania's voice, calls Cobweb's name in the same way as before'

Cobweb.

The whole group comes to life, replicating her physical movement and voice, repeating the sequence of 'Cobweb' and 'Ready' three times.

When they have finished the group return to standing.

MUSTARDSEED

Another actor assumes the starting shape of Mustardseed with clenched fists, knees bent, feet together, ready to explode.

The leader plays the voice of Titania and calls Mustardseed's name, making long vowel sounds as if calling into another world.

Mustardseed.

Mustardseed bursts into life, running as fast as possible on the spot, burning herself into the ground and repeating her name three times as quickly as possible. She is an explosion of energy, emanating from the scalding heat of mustard. Her movements are tiny and fast, running on the spot, fists clenched, making herself as minuscule as a tiny, hot seed and speaking her name as fast and high as she can.

Mustardseed Mustardseed Mustardseed.

And then with the same speed and energy she says:

Ready ready ready.

As soon as Mustardseed's demonstration is over, the leader invites the whole group to copy and everyone assumes Mustardseed's starting shape, clenched fists, knees bent, and feet together, ready to explode.

When the whole group are ready to play, the leader using Titania's voice, calls Mustardseeds's name in the same way as before:

Mustardseed.

The whole group comes to life, replicating the physical movement and voice, repeating the sequence of 'Mustardseed' and 'Ready' three times.

When they have finished they return to standing.

PEASEBLOSSOM

Another actor assumes the starting shape of Peaseblossom, knees bent low, hands together in prayer, body and arms curled up tight as if ready to be born.

The leader plays the voice of Titania and calls Peaseblossom's name, making long vowel sounds as if calling into another world.

Peaseblossom.

Peaseblossom slowly unfurls into life, feet stationary, her upper body, arms and hands emerging from the starting position as if she is a long branch of blossom twisting, curling and swaying up toward the sun. Her movements are flowing and sensuous, emanating from summer blossom. Each repetition of her name represents the budding of new, fresh blossom.

She speaks the first part of her name, shifting from low to high in register as she is unfolding:

Pease ...

She makes a small bursting movement as her hands separate above her head as if she has emerged into the sunshine saying in a high register:

Blossom.

Stretching her body, arms and hands upward she says:

Ready.

As soon as Peaseblossoms's demonstration is over, the leader invites the whole group to copy and everybody assumes the starting shape of Peaseblossom, knees bent low, hands together in prayer, body and arms curled up tight as if ready to be born.

When the whole group are ready to play, the leader using Titania's voice, calls Peaseblossoms's name in the same way as before.

Peaseblossom.

The whole group comes to life, replicating the physical movement and voice, repeating the sequence of 'Peaseblossom' and 'Ready' three times.

When they have finished, they shake out their bodies and take a breathing space.

Playing with the children

Whilst you are playing around the circle offer the children hands-on support if they find the transformations difficult, supporting them to experience how it feels to change their bodies. Once all four fairies have been demonstrated as above, split up into pairs or small groups around the room to explore the transformations further.

Work with the children according to their needs. If they are able to copy you as a mirror, encourage them to do so and if they need greater assistance, gently work with their bodies so they begin to experience how the transformations feel. Encourage them to explore the distinct physical and vocal differences of the four fairies, ensuring that the act of animating these tiny creatures is as otherworldly and dreamlike as it can be.

Working through the journey of all four in order provides a transcendent physical experience as you change from one to the other beginning with the power of Moth through to the wiry Cobweb to the unpredictable Mustardseed and finishing with the sensuousness of Peaseblossom. Allow their surreal nature to heighten your demonstrations and encourage the children to copy you, stretching their own physicality and vocal range as well as their imaginative life.

When you have explored the game to its fullest possibility come back to the circle and share.

What's your name?

Once the fairies have arrived in the bower, Bottom asks them their names, requesting that they scratch his donkey head. 'What's your name' focuses on turn taking, providing an opportunity to explore the difference between asking a question, giving an answer and waiting your turn. This 'lesson' is embedded in the game, which with a donkey asking questions and a fairy giving answers is surreal and pleasurable. For this demonstration one person plays all four fairies.

Demonstration

Before playing memorize these lines

> Your name, honest gentleman?
> Good Master.

Two actors are in the circle. One is Bottom with his donkey head, buckteeth, hands as ears and twitchy nose. The other actor plays the fairy.

The fairy uses the physical and vocal transformations from the previous game.

Bottom is sitting in the centre of the circle about three paces away from the fairy who assumes Moth's starting shape.

To begin Bottom makes eye contact with the fairy and says:

> Your name, honest gentleman?

The fairy comes to life as Moth, and using Moth's voice and gesture she says:

> Moth. Ready.

To which Bottom replies:

> Good master Moth.

The fairy now takes the starting shape of Cobweb, smacking her lips.

Bottom says:

Your name, honest gentleman?

The fairy comes to life as Cobweb, and using Cobweb's voice and gestures, she says:

Cob...b...b... web...b...b... Ready.

To which Bottom replies:

Good master Cobweb.

The fairy now takes the starting shape of Mustardseed, bursting to run fast on the spot and Bottom says:

Your name, honest gentleman?

Fairy bursts into life as Mustardseed, and using Mustardseed's voice and gestures, she says:

Mustardseed, Mustardseed, Mustardseed. Ready, ready, ready.

To which Bottom replies:

Good master Mustardseed.

The fairy now takes the starting shape of Peaseblossom, and Bottom says:

Your name, honest gentleman?

Now the fairy comes to life as Peaseblossom, and using Peaseblossom's voice and gestures she says:

Peaseblossom. Ready.

To which Bottom replies:

Good master Peaseblossom.

Playing with the children

Modify this game to suit the child's cognitive abilities. If they are struggling with the fairy transformations, allow them to choose one fairy to play (it's usually Mustardseed) so they can concentrate fully on the turn taking. The target of the game is to explore the difference between asking and answering. You can modify the questions to this simpler version:

Bottom: What's your name?
Fairy: Mustardseed
Bottom: Hello Mustardseed

Ensure that you continue to explore the characterizations of the donkey and fairy to keep the game from becoming too 'normal'. Encourage the child to play both parts, swapping back and forth between asking and answering, practising the natural inflections for both. You may want to elicit the help of another adult or child to play with you, so you can partner up with the child and as a duo fully immerse yourselves in one task at a time, first as the donkey asking the questions and then as the fairy giving the answers.

When you are ready, return to the circle to share.

Adding 'I must scratch'

Bottom asks the fairies to scratch his donkey head and each fairy by turn obliges him. This version adds even more surreal images to Bottom's dream, stretching the children's language skills and imaginative powers.

Demonstration

Before playing memorize these lines

> Your name, honest gentleman?
> Scratch my head
> I must scratch

Two actors are in the circle. One is Bottom with his donkey head, buckteeth, hands as ears and twitchy nose. The other actor is the fairy who assumes Moth's starting shape.

Bottom is sitting in the centre of the circle about three paces away from the fairy.

To begin Bottom makes eye contact with the fairy and says:

Your name, honest gentleman?

Fairy comes to life as Moth, making Moth's physical gesture, and using Moth's voice she says:

Moth. Ready.

To which Bottom replies:

Scratch my head, Moth.

Moth stretches her arms in front of her and mimes a scratching action with her fingers, repeating it three times.

Bottom is very happy and scratching his own head three times says:

I must scratch.

The fairy now takes the starting shape of Cobweb, smacking her lips.

Bottom says:

Your name, honest gentleman?

The fairy comes to life as Cobweb, and using Cobweb's voice and gestures she says:

Cob...b...b... web...b...b... Ready.

To which Bottom replies:

Scratch my head, Cobweb.

Cobweb stretches her arms in front of her and mimes a scratching action with her fingers, repeating it three times.

Bottom is very happy and scratching his own head three times says:

I must scratch.

The fairy now takes the starting position of Mustardseed and Bottom says:

Your name, honest gentleman?

The fairy comes to life as Mustardseed, and using Mustardseed's voice and gestures she says:

Mustardseed, Mustardseed, Mustardseed. Ready, ready, ready.

To which Bottom replies:

Scratch my head, Mustardseed.

Mustardseed stretches her arms in front of her and mimes a scratching action with her fingers, repeating it three times.
Bottom is very happy and scratching his own head three times says:

I must scratch.

The fairy comes to life as Peaseblossom, and using Peaseblossom's voice and gestures, she says:

Peaseblossom. Ready.

To which Bottom replies:

Scratch my head, Peaseblossom.

Peaseblossom stretches her arms in front of her and mimes a scratching action with her fingers, repeating it three times.
Bottom is very happy and scratching his own head three times says:

I must scratch.

Playing with the children

Encourage the children to fully inhabit the rhythm of three scratches every time the donkey and the fairy make their movements, so that the game has a pulsing, flowing rhythm to it, providing the children with a rhythmic framework to lock onto whilst enhancing the dreamlike feeling of the game. As before, if the child struggles with making the transformations allow them to play just one fairy in order to immerse themselves in dialogue with the donkey.

When you have repeated the game several times, come back to the circle to share.

I have had a dream

> I have had a most rare vision, I have had a dream, past the wit of man to say what dream it was. Man is but an ass, if he go about to expound this dream. Methought I was – there is no man can tell what. Methought I was, and methought I had, but man is but a patched fool, if he will offer to say what methought I had. The eye of man hath not heard, the ear of man hath not seen, man's hand is not able to taste, his tongue to conceive, nor his heart to report what my dream was.
>
> *(A Midsummer Night's Dream, IV, i, 214–23)*

When the spell is lifted from Titania's eyes, she sees clearly that Bottom is a man with a donkey's head and revolted by the sight of him, returns to her fairy kingdom. Puck removes the donkey's head from Bottom and when he wakes, he describes his night's adventure as a dream.

This game has the effect of isolating the senses, providing the opportunity to focus solely on one sensory experience at a time. This deepens the children's sensory awareness within an attentive listening silence, offering an experience of profound concentration through Bottom's upside-down world.

Demonstration/playing with the children

Before playing memorize these lines

> The eye of man has not heard,
> the ear of man has not seen,

man's hand is not able to taste,
his tongue to conceive,
nor his heart to report what my dream was.

With everyone sitting around the circle, begin to speak Bottom's speech as below, asking the children to join you after each phrase and explore each sensation. Alternatively an actor assumes the character of Bottom and speaks the lines, while you as leader ask the questions. Both versions work equally well.

Each time you say 'Lets try', encourage the whole group to follow your instruction. Allow as much time as feels comfortable for the children to explore their senses in silence before moving on to the next one.

Bottom: I have had a dream
          The eye of man has not heard
Leader: Can you listen with your eyes? Let's try

Encourage the children to use their eyes to listen to the sounds of the room; creating a 'listening silence'. They can cover their ears if they choose. It's interesting that many children increase their eye contact with others around the circle during this stage, as if their 'hearing eyes' cannot be seen. After a minute or so ask the children to finish, tell them what you heard and allow them to offer up their experience. Move on to the next stage.

Bottom: The ear of man has not seen
Leader: Can you see with your ears? Let's close our eyes and try

Ask the children to close their eyes for this second stage to explore what they can 'see with their ears'. Focusing entirely on your own ears whilst your eyes are closed and at the same time trying to see creates an intense experience of concentrated listening, many children rock from side to side and some start to hum or sing. After a minute or so, ask the children to finish, tell them what you saw and allow them to offer up their experience. Move on to the next stage.

Bottom: His hand is not able to taste
Leader: Can you taste with your hands? Let's try

Ensure that the children isolate their fingers and hands and that as far as possible nothing else in the body moves. Encourage them to move their hands and fingers gently as if their fingertips were doing the tasting. Many children close their eyes for this stage, adding a further dimension to their sensory awareness. Allow an intense silence to ensue and after a minute or so, ask the children to finish, tell them what you tasted and allow them to offer up their experience. In my experience the majority of children 'taste air'. Move on to the next stage.

Bottom: His tongue to conceive
Leader: Can you understand the world with your tongue? Let's try

Encourage the children to isolate the movements of their tongue, rolling it, stretching it and varying the tempo with which they move it. You can liken this to the way people use their tongue when they are concentrating very hard trying to solve a problem; conceiving the world in a new way. After a minute or so, ask the children to finish, tell them what you understood and allow them to offer up their experience. This is the most ambiguous of the five stages and although it may yield the smallest response, do not be tempted to miss it out. Move on to the next stage.

Bottom: Nor his heart to report what my dream was.
Leader: Can you speak from the heart? Let's try

Encourage the children to focus on their hearts, keeping completely silent and yet wanting to speak. Their eyes can be opened or closed. Some children place their hands on their hearts and some beat out a heartbeat, connecting the exercise with the heartbeat circles. The aim of this last stage is to explore the desire to speak without making sound; this is an exploration of the longing to express feelings. Give them a minute or so and ask them to finish, tell them what you felt in your heart, and allow them to offer up their experience.

The mind's eye questions

The mind's eye questions act as a bridge between the games explored so far and the demands of the games in the next chapter. So far, the children have been asked to make imaginative transformations by copying the actors, whilst the next chapter offers them a chance to explore the concept of playing a part independently using their mind's eye. Many of the children claim there is no such thing as the mind's eye, demanding proof of its existence. These four questions and their answers can serve as verification.

Within the questions is the opportunity for the children to act out their dreams. This is a potentially powerful exercise, and depending on the children's cognitive abilities, can be returned to as often as appropriate. With my original group of children, I set aside ten minutes each session, turning the circle into a 'dream circle' in which with the assistance of the actors, the children had the opportunity to physically embody their dreams.

Demonstration/playing with the children

Everyone is sitting around the circle and the leader asks the questions; they can also be shared between the leader and the actors. During the second question the leader and actors all join in to act out the children's dreams.

FIRST QUESTION

> Do you dream?

The answer to this question does not need to be elaborate; yes, no or maybe is all you're after, it's just a starting point. If the children are reluctant to answer, don't push them, tell them that you dream, and ask the actors and adults to answer the question as well. There is usually a child who insists that he or she never dreams to which you can answer something along the lines of 'How interesting, listen to my other questions and tell me what you think.' When you've confirmed that you as a group (or at least the majority) do dream, move on to the next question.

SECOND QUESTION

> What do you *see* in your dreams?

Ask this with an emphasis on the seeing. Encourage the children to offer up images and narratives from their dreams and after a few children have shared, get up on your feet in the circle and invite the children to act out their dream with you. If they are shy of 'acting' they can be the narrator and you can be the 'dream'. (Initially the dreams often involve 'lights' so be prepared to pretend be a light, however you may do this.) The actors also get up and invite children to play; the atmosphere is good-humoured and creative. If no child offers their dreams initially, you and the actors offer yours. Act the dream without any preparation, nothing should be impossible to realize and vitally it should be fun.

This is the longest part of the four questions, the most interactive and potentially transformative for the children. Keep the dreams short, sharing a small moment of acting with the child. Allow as many children as you like to share; if they are willing, they should have a go. Once children who are eager have acted out their dream, move on to the next question.

THIRD QUESTION

When you're dreaming are your eyes opened or closed?

Most children will answer that their eyes are closed. Some may answer that they sleep (and do or do not dream) with their eyes open and some that their parents have found them sleepwalking. All the answers are, of course, valid. Ultimately, you should agree that most if not all people dream with their eyes closed and that if their eyes are open during sleep they can still see things that aren't there. This leads to the fourth and final question.

FOURTH QUESTION

If your eyes are closed when you are sleeping, how can you see your dreams?

For children who insist they sleep with their eyes open you can say:

If your eyes are open when you are sleeping how can you see things that aren't there?

Ask them to recall the specific dreams that you have acted out, saying something along the lines of 'how did you see the monster falling through your window if your eyes were closed?' In my experience the children offer up all sorts of ideas. A common train of thought is that we have TV screens in our brains, which get switched on when we go to sleep and another common answer is that there are screens inside our eyes that can 'turn inside out'. Screens and TVs may feature heavily in the answers and some children offer up the idea of *imagination*, but are unable to explain how it makes you see.

Allow the difficulty of illuminating the workings of imagination to continue for a few minutes and finally introduce the mind's eye; an eye more powerful than your two regular eyes can ever be.

If appropriate, I introduce them to Shakespeare; a writer who lived many centuries ago and first coined the phrase 'the mind's eye'. This may or not be relevant for the group; what is important is that the children engage on a personal level with their own mind's eye. Once you have introduced it, encourage the children to explore the idea of seeing with the mind's eye as often as you like, using the phrase as part of your teaching, ensuring that the children continue to make a connection with their unconscious, and through the drama games and the dream circle they are given the opportunity to express their interior lives.

Chapter 4

The mechanicals

Let the audience look to their eyes, I will move storms
(A Midsummer Night's Dream, I, ii, 24–5)

There are six mechanicals in the play, one of whom – Bottom – has been at the centre of the games so far. Each of the mechanicals has a profession and they are meeting in the forest to rehearse a play. These next games explore the character of Bottom and his five friends in more detail.

These games have a different quality from the games of fairyland just as the mechanicals themselves feel very different within the play, speaking only in prose, whereas Titania, Puck and the lovers speak only in verse. The games seem simple on the surface, but like the character of Bottom, their effect and resonance are profound.

Using the concept of the mind's eye these games tackle the imaginative leap necessary to become another person – to play a part.

The games

- My mind's eye
- Playing a part
- You must play Pyramus
- *Pyramus and Thisbe* script

The characters

- Nick Bottom, the Weaver
- Francis Flute, the Bellows-Mender
- Peter Quince, the Carpenter
- Snug, the joiner
- Robin Starveling, the Tailor
- Tom Snout, the Tinker

The targets

- Making an imaginative transformation.
- Exploring the mind's eye.
- Playing a part
- Building a character

My mind's eye

Making the imaginative leap necessary to 'become' another person is often a new concept for the children. This first game explores the process of 'changing into another person' allowing the children to physically experience the difference between seeing with their real eyes and using their mind's eye. The heart of the game provides the opportunity to use their mind's eye as a stimulus for moving their bodies.

The game uses repetitive movements and phrases to bring the six mechanicals to life, and the leader uses a series of instructions and commands which remain the same no matter which mechanical is introduced. I use the character of Flute the Bellows-Mender for the first demonstration followed by a description of body shape, gesture, phrase and voice for the remaining five mechanicals. The leader uses the actors' own names during the game, here I've used Tom and Joan.

The instructions and commands may appear arduous at first, but the game in fact takes very little time and the children enjoy the order and discipline of its structure.

Demonstration

Before playing memorize the body shapes, movements, words and voices for the mechanicals. You do not have to demonstrate all six in one session, chose two or three to start with.

To begin everyone is sitting around the circle. Two actors opposite each other stand up, remaining where they are so the whole group can see them clearly. One actor is Flute the Bellows-Mender and the other is the 'camera'. Both actors make eye contact to begin.

Leader: Instruction: Joan, on my command, I would like you to close your eyes.
Command: Joan, close.

She closes her eyes and waits.

Leader: Instruction: Tom, on my command I would like you to
make the shape of Flute the Bellows-Mender.
Command: Tom, make the shape of Flute the Bellows-
Mender.

Tom transforms his body into the body shape of Flute mending
bellows; cheeks puffed out, arms bent as if holding bellows, legs
apart and knees bent. He stays as still as a statue until he is told to
come to life.

Leader: Instruction: Joan, on my command I would like you to
open your eyes and take in every detail of Flute as if you
were a camera.
Command: Joan, open.

She opens her eyes and looks at every detail of Flute, as though she
were a camera. She is using her real eyes.

Leader: Instruction: Joan, on my command I would like you to
close your eyes and keeping them closed, see Flute in your
mind's eye.
Command: Joan, close.

She closes her eyes. She is seeing with her mind's eye.

Leader: Instruction: Joan, keeping your eyes closed, on my
command I would like you to copy the shape of Flute with
your body.
Command: Joan, copy.

Using her mind's eye and keeping her real eyes closed, she copies the
body shape of Flute as exactly as possible. When she has finished she
keeps her eyes shut and remains still, having created her reflection
of Flute. This stage is at the heart of the exercise – using the mind's
eye as stimulus for moving the body.

Leader: Instruction: Joan, on my command open your eyes, keep
your body still and see your picture.
Command: Joan, open.

Maintaining her body shape she opens her eyes and looks at Flute, as if seeing a reflection of herself. This provides a POE in the game. (You can finish the game here in a simple version)

Leader: Instruction: Tom, on my command bring Flute to life with movement.
Command: Tom bring Flute to life.

Tom starts to move his body with rhythm, bending and stretching his knees and arms as if he were testing bellows and simultaneously puffing air out of his cheeks. He repeats this movement three times.

Leader: Instruction : Joan, on my command copy Flute's movements.
Command: Joan, copy.

Joan comes to life and copies the movements of Flute.

Leader: Instruction: Tom, on my command speak Flute's words.
Command: Flute, speak.

Tom puts his hand to his chin and says in a deep voice 'I have a beard coming'

Leader: Instruction: Joan, on my command copy Flute's words.
Command: Joan, copy.

Joan comes to life and copies the words and voice of Flute.

Leader: Instruction: Tom, on my command bring Flute to life and speak Flute's words.
Command: Flute, come to life and speak.

Tom makes the movements, repeating them three times and then speaks Flut'es words.

Leader: Instruction: Joan, on my command copy Flute's movements and speak Flute's words.
Command: Joan, copy.

Joan comes to life and copies the movements of Flute as exactly as possible, followed by his words.

The actors sit back down.

Now invite the children and actors to stand up all together around the outside of the circle. One actor plays a different Mechanical from the list below and the whole group become cameras. Begin straightaway with the game fresh in everyone's memory, repeating the same commands and instructions from above whilst using the new Mechanical. When giving the instructions and commands, replace 'Joan' with the name 'Cameras' to address the whole group.

Body shape, movement, words and voice for the remaining mechanicals

SNUG THE JOINER

Body shape:	Standing, knees slightly bent, hands out in front of him as if holding and joining together two heavy pieces of wood.
Movement:	Very slowly turning the wood with his hands, until the two pieces join, vocalizing the exertion of his energy.
Words:	'I am slow of study.'
Voice:	Low and slow.

ROBIN STARVELING THE TAILOR

Body shape:	Standing, legs tightly together, hands and fingers as if threading a needle, eyes screwed up, as if needing spectacles.
Movement:	Threading the needle and then pricking his finger, he makes a little 'Oh' of surprise.
Words:	'I fear it I promise you.'
Voice:	High and timid.

TOM SNOUT THE TINKER

Body shape:	Standing, arms stretched up as if holding a pan with one hand and tapping it with a spoon with the other.
Movement:	Tapping the pan with a spoon.
Words:	'Tink tink tink tink tink.'
Voice:	High and quiet.

PETER QUINCE THE CARPENTER

Body shape: Standing, hands as if holding a saw and piece of wood.
Movement: Sawing the wood with long movements, making the sound of the saw 'zzz-zzz zzz-zzz zzz-zzz donk' as the wood falls to the floor.
Words: 'Oh most happy day.'
Voice: Confident and loud.

NICK BOTTOM THE WEAVER

Body shape: Standing as if weaving a basket.
Movement: Hands and arms move forward and backwards as if weaving. He makes large expansive movements, saying 'Thread that, clackety clack'.
Words: 'A very fine piece of work I assure you.'
Voice: Confident and loud.

Playing with the children

The aim of the game is to encourage the children to use their mind's eye as stimulus to move their bodies. The simple version is to finish the game once the children have done this, when they have copied the shape and opened their eyes to see the reflection. Whichever version you play, give the children encouragement and support from the moment they close their eyes, through their exploration of the copying and until they have opened them again; they are likely to feel particularly vulnerable with their eyes closed. The repetitive style of the instructions and commands provides a structure for the children within which they can feel increasingly secure and confident. Your tone should be assertive enough to hold their attention, bur remain friendly and warm to assure them that this is indeed a game to be enjoyed.

Ensure that each body shape, movement, phrase and voice is playful and slightly exaggerated, heightening the child's experience. Play the game at a good flowing pace, each stage lasting just long enough to be absorbing and then moving on to the next so that the whole exercise feels smooth.

Once the game is established invite the children to take turns creating the mechanicals, sticking to Shakespeare's words and inventing their own body shape, gesture and voice. It is empowering for the child to see everyone transforming their bodies into the body shape of the mechanical they have created. Play the game until the children have all had a chance to create a version for everyone to copy.

Playing a part

Within the play the mechanicals are putting on a performance of *Pyramus and Thisbe*. Peter Quince is the director, Bottom is to play Pyramus, Flute is to play Thisbe, Snout, the Wall, Starveling, the Moon and Snug, the Lion.

The very idea of playing a part can be strange and unfamiliar for the children. This game, made of introductions and transformations, offers a clear structure within which to explore this potentially confusing concept. Played as a solo experience, using the building blocks of body shape, gesture, phrase and voice from the previous game, the player transforms herself into one of the mechanicals and then makes a second transformation into the role the mechanical is playing in *Pyramus and Thisbe*.

The effect of the mechanical's journey is light-hearted and pleasurable for the children, whilst the more serious endeavour of playing a part is being explored. Peter Quince is not included, as he does not play a part in *Pyramus and Thisbe*.

Demonstration

Before playing memorize the body shapes, movements, words and voices for the mechanicals. I have listed all six but you do not have to demonstrate them in one session; choose two or three to start with.

Everyone is sitting around the circle. One actor stands, remaining where he is so the whole group can see him clearly. He chooses Flute the Bellows-Mender.

FLUTE THE BELLOWS-MENDER

To begin he introduces himself:

I'm Tom.

Next he says which mechanical he's playing:

And I'm playing Flute the Bellows-Mender.

And he transforms himself into Flute, making the body shape and the rhythmic gesture of mending the bellows from the previous game.

Using Flute's low voice, he speaks his phrase:

I have a beard coming,

Staying in Flute's body shape and using Flute's low voice, he introduces himself again saying which part he is playing in *Pyramus and Thisbe:*

I'm Flute and I'm playing Thisbe.

Now he transforms into Thisbe.

His hands become fluttery, his body trembling and his voice becomes very high. He speaks:

Asleep my love?

This transformation from the manly low-voiced Flute into the feminine trembling high-voiced Thisbe is dramatic and humorous creating a POE.

The actor sits back down.

An actor stands and chooses Snug the Joiner. The structure of the game remains exactly the same; only the characteristics differ.

SNUG THE JOINER

First the actor introduces herself:

I'm Joan.

Next she says which mechanical she's playing:

And I'm playing Snug the Joiner.

And then she transforms herself into Snug, making the body shape and the rhythmic gesture of joining her two pieces of wood from the previous game.

Using Snug's quiet voice she speaks her phrase:

> I am slow of study.

Staying in Snug's body shape, and using Snug's quiet voice she introduces herself again saying which part she is playing in *Pyramus and Thisbe:*

> I'm Snug and I'm playing the Lion.

Now she transforms into the Lion.

Her hands become paws with claws; her body and arms ready to pounce like a lion and her voice as deep and powerful as possible. She speaks:

> Rough, rage, roar.

This transformation from the timid Snug into the roaring Lion is dramatic and humorous creating a POE.

The actor sits back down.

An actor stands and chooses Bottom the Weaver. The structure of the game remains exactly the same; only the characteristics differ.

NICK BOTTOM THE WEAVER

First the actor introduces herself:

> I'm Joan.

Next she says which mechanical she's playing:

> And I'm playing Bottom the Weaver.

And then she transforms herself into Bottom, making the body shape and the rhythmic gesture of weaving from the previous game.

Using Bottom's confident voice, she speaks his phrase:

> A very fine piece of work I assure you.

Staying in Bottom's body shape, and using his confident loud voice she introduces herself again saying which part she is playing in *Pyramus and Thisbe:*

I'm Bottom and I'm playing Pyramus.

Now she transforms into Pyramus.

She takes the stance of a romantic knight, with a sword drawn high above her head, about to stab herself in the heart. On the last 'die' she will fall to the floor. Her voice passionate and resonant, she speaks:

Die, die, die, die, die.

This transformation from the confident Bottom into the passionate Pyramus is as if his enthusiasm is inevitable and must pour out of him, creating a POE.

The actor sits back down.

An actor stands and chooses Robin Starveling the Tailor. The structure of the game remains exactly the same; only the characteristics differ.

ROBIN STARVELING THE TAILOR

First the actor introduces himself:

I'm Tom.

Next he says which mechanical he's playing:

And I'm playing Robin Starveling the Tailor.

And then he transforms himself into Starveling, making the body shape and the rhythmic gesture of sewing and pricking his finger from the previous game.

Using Starveling's quiet voice, he then speaks his phrase:

I fear it, I promise you.

Staying in Starveling's body shape, and using his quiet voice he introduces himself again saying which part he is playing in *Pyramus and Thisbe*:

I'm Starveling and I'm playing Moonshine.

Now he transforms himself into the Moon.

He raises his arms above his head and leans to one side as if to represent a crescent moon. His voice is positive, shining with confidence.

> Myself the man i' the moon doth seem to be.

This transformation from the timid Starveling into the shining Moon is as if a new character has just been born, creating a POE.

The actor sits back down.

An actor stands and chooses Tom Snout the Tinker. The structure of the game remains exactly the same; only the characteristics differ.

TOM SNOUT THE TINKER

First the actor introduces himself:

> I'm Tom.

Next he says which mechanical he's playing:

> And I'm playing Tom Snout the Tinker.

And then he transforms himself into Tom Snout, making the body shape and the rhythmic gesture of tapping the pots and pans, from the previous game.

Using Tom Snout's quiet, high voice, he then speaks his phrase:

> Tink, tink, tink, tink, tink.

Staying in Tom Snout's body shape, and using his high, quiet voice he introduces himself again saying which part he is playing in *Pyramus and Thisbe*

> I'm Tom Snout and I'm playing The Wall.

Now he transforms himself into the Wall.

He bends his knees, arms out in front of him, making himself as square and upright as possible as with a very low voice and a slow, weary delivery. He speaks:

Wall so ....Wall go.

This transformation from the high-voiced, enthusiastic Tinker to the low-voiced weary Wall is humorous and creates the POE.

The actor sits back down.

Playing with the children

Play in pairs or small groups around the room, and let the children choose which mechanical they are going to play. Practise line-by-line making sure the child understands and owns each phase of the game. Depending on their cognitive levels they may need to copy your every move or at the other end of the spectrum they may make their own versions of the mechanical. Stick to Shakespeare's language but allow them to invent their own body shapes, gestures and voices.

This deliberately slow game has energy within it; its thoughtful pace offers the children the chance to grasp the idea of playing a part whilst the transformative power of Shakespeare's characters keeps the game alive. Allow the children to take their time over each phase but at the same time encourage an intensified style so that the children are genuinely transforming their bodies and voices, exploring the changes they can create within themselves.

The initial introduction of oneself should be plain and simple. The first transformation into the mechanical is a burst of physical activity and your voice is immediately changed. This level of heightened activity is then built upon for the second transformation, which is even more dynamic, as if there is a pulsing need for the changes to burst out of you; with each transformation a new level of transcendence can be experienced.

When you have repeated the game several times, come back to share with the whole group.

You must play Pyramus

Bottom has the desire to play every part in *Pyramus and Thisbe*, believing himself to be the best actor in the troupe. As Peter Quince gives out the parts Bottom constantly interrupts, claiming each part for himself. 'You must play Pyramus' brings that scene to life. Ensure that you have fully explored the last two games before you try this one, otherwise it will be difficult and confusing.

The repetition of the phrases makes the game easy and enjoyable for the children to play and encourages them to enjoy taking turns. The game provides the opportunity for the children to develop ownership of one part, using the building blocks of the previous exercises. For the demonstration I will assume six actors are present, you can modify this according to your needs.

Demonstration

Before playing, memorize all these lines

Six actors stand, remaining where they are so the whole group can see them clearly. They introduce themselves, each assuming a body shape of one of the mechanicals, which they keep for the whole game. When they speak, they stay in their place around the circle, using their mechanical's gesture and voice. When Bottom speaks, he is able to act out everyone's part, changing his body and voice accordingly. The script is as follows:

Quince:	Bottom the Weaver
Bottom:	Here, Peter Quince
Quince:	You must play Pyramus
Bottom:	What is Pyramus?
Quince:	A lover, that kills himself
Bottom:	*(as Pyramus)* Die, die, die, die die!
Quince:	Flute, the Bellows-Mender
Flute:	Here, Peter Quince
Quince:	You must play Thisbe
Flute:	I have a beard coming
Bottom:	Let me play Thisbe
	(as Thisbe) Asleep my love?
Everyone:	No! You must play Pyramus
Quince:	Snug the joiner
Snug:	Here Peter Quince
Quince:	You must play the Lion
Snug:	I am slow of study
Bottom:	Let me play Lion
	(as Lion) Rough, Rage, Roar
Everyone:	No! You must play Pyramus
Quince:	Tom Snout, the Tinker
Snout:	Here Peter Quince
Quince:	You must play the wall

Bottom:	Let me play the wall
	(as Wall) BOOM!
Everyone:	No! You must play Pyramus
Quince:	Robin Starveling the tailor
Starveling:	Here Peter Quince
Quince:	You must play the Moonshine
Starveling:	I fear it I promise you
Bottom:	Let me play Moonshine
	(as Moonshine) Shine!
Everyone:	No! You must play Pyramus

Playing with the children

Once the game has been demonstrated all the way through, begin by practising the key line altogether. 'No! You must play Pyramus'. Repeat it quietly, each time increasing with intensity, though not volume, creating a small POE with each repetition.

Now invite the children to stand up, choosing which mechanical they will play and joining the actors in pairs or small groups around the circle. Play the whole scene again, everyone standing at the outside of the circle so that they may see each other, the actors prompting the children with the words and movements of their specific mechanical when it is their turn. Build on the work you have explored in the previous games, ensuring that the children embody the gesture and voice of their mechanical, transforming themselves physically and vocally.

Once you have played all together, split off in pairs or small groups to practise the words and movements, using the building blocks of the previous two games to build the child's confidence as they take on their part. Work with the children according to their needs and after repeating the exercise several times return to the circle for a final time to play the scene.

Pyramus and Thisbe

At the end of *A Midsummer Night's Dream* the mechanicals perform *Pyramus and Thisbe* to great acclaim. This short version is manageable for the children once they have explored all the games in this chapter. Give each child a part to play, encouraging them to feel a sense of ownership and let them practise their part with an actor as a pair or a small group. Use your prompting skills to teach the language to the children; some of the lines will already be familiar through the previous three games. I have not given precise physical gesture for each moment; this is a chance for the actors and children to be creative together.

Allow time for practising this short play but beware of letting it dominate too much within a workshop. At best, you can work on it over time alongside other games as a culmination of the work you have explored in this section.

Using prompting, the short play should feel like an extension of the games, the actors playing with the children together. This is not to be viewed as a chance for the children to 'perform' by themselves but rather a chance for everyone to share the skills explored so far, children and adults playing together.

The roles of Pyramus and Thisbe have far more lines than the others. Allow as many children as you like to play these two parts, this is not a case of the most 'talented child getting a big part'. I once had a whole class engaged in playing the 'dying Pyramus', every one of them transformed, committed and loving it; it was a great example of how Shakespeare accommodates the children. Conversely if these parts are too challenging, the actors playing the parts can speak the words, prompting the children at key moments as they go along.

The leader and all the actors involved should know all the parts.

Characters

- Peter Quince
- Pyramus
- Thisbe
- Wall
- Moonshine
- Lion

Enter Peter Quince.

Quince: Part One, at the Wall.

Enter Wall.
She stands with both arms stretched out in front of her, fingers closed together.
Enter Pyramus and Thisbe from opposite sides of Wall.

Pyramus:	Oh wall, oh wall, oh sweet and lovely wall,
	Chink ... Blink
Wall:	*(opens her fingers apart)* Zing!
Pyramus:	Thanks courteous wall.
Thisbe:	Oh wall.
Pyramus:	I see a voice!
	Oh kiss me through the hole of this vile wall.

Pyramus and Thisbe kiss the fingers of Wall

Thisbe:	I kiss the wall's hole and not your lips at all.
Pyramus:	Meet me at Ninny's tomb straight away.
Thisbe:	I come, I come, I come without delay.

Pyramus and Thisbe exit

Wall:	Wall so ... Wall go.

Wall exits
Enter Peter Quince

Quince:	Part two. At Ninny's tomb

Exit Peter Quince.
Enter Moonshine and Lion.
Moonshine stands in a curved crescent, Lion hides behind, ready to pounce.

Moonshine:	Myself the man i' the moon do seem to be.

Enter Thisbe, wearing a scarf.

Thisbe:	This is Ninny's tomb, where is my love?

Lion appears from behind Moon.

Lion:	Rough ... Rage ... Roar!

Thisbe cries out and exits.
Lion plays with Thisbe's scarf.

Lion: Rough, rage, roar, rough, rage, roar, rough rage, roar.

Lion exits, leaving Thisbe's scarf on stage.
Pyramus enters.

Pyramus: Sweet moon, I thank you for your sunny beams
                I thank you moon for shining here so bright.

Pyramus sees Thisbe's scarf.

Pyramus: But stay oh spite, but mark poor knight
                What dreadful dole is here.
                Eyes do you see, how can this be?
                Oh dainty duck, oh dear.

Pyramus draws his sword

Pyramus: Now I am dead, now I am fled.
                My soul is in the sky.
                Now die, die, die, die, die

He falls to the floor. Dead.
Thisbe enters. She sees the body of Pyramus.

Thisbe: Asleep my love?
                What dead my dove?
                Oh Pyramus arise.
                Dead, dead?
                A tomb must cover your sweet eyes.

Thisbe takes the sword and stabs herself

Thisbe: Come blade, my breast imbrue.
                Farewell friends.
                Thus Thisbe ends.
                Adieu.
                Adieu.
                Adieu.

Thisbe dies.

Chapter 5

The lovers

The course of true love ne'er did run smooth.
(*A Midsummer Night's Dream*, I, i, 136)

There are two pairs of lovers in the forest whose love lives become tangled when Puck tricks their eyes with the same 'love Juice' that was used on Titania. Their story is the most complicated in the play and accordingly these games are more complex, with challenging tasks of language, reasoning and physicality. The work builds on the foundations established by the games of fairyland, offering further exploration for making eye contact, improving spatial awareness and developing language skills.

The games

- More faces
- Throwing the face, body and voice
- Puck's petals
- Lysander's trance
- Lovers' trance

The characters

- Helena
- Hermia
- Demetrius
- Lysander
- Puck

The targets

- Making eye contact
- Improving facial expressiveness
- Improving spatial awareness
- Developing sensory awareness

More faces

This game uses the framework of 'Throwing the face' (p. 19) to introduce the four lovers, allowing the children to practise four new faces within the structure of a familiar game and simultaneously acquaint themselves with the four new characters.

Demonstration

Before playing prepare and memorize these faces

- Helena has a jealous face
- Demetrius has a frustrated face
- Hermia has a lovesick face
- Lysander has a thoughtful face.

HELENA'S JEALOUS FACE

Immediately after the 'Hello heartbeats' with everyone still sitting around the circle, an actor assumes the jealous face of Helena. This face is pinched, unhappy and turning to one side 'in a huff'. Once the face is established, an actor on the opposite side of the circle becomes the 'catcher', ready to 'catch' the face of Helena.

Slowly say '1, 2, 3 Throw' at the end of which Helena 'throws' her face across the circle toward the 'catcher'. The action from Helena should be as if a mask is being flung from her face, requiring physical and vocal effort. The catcher immediately assumes Helena's jealous face with an element of surprise as if it has landed from nowhere. He then keeps the face energized, almost squealing with jealousy until you instruct him to throw it again.

Now choose another actor or child to be the 'catcher' and instruct the new Helena to get ready to throw the face. When both players are ready to 'throw' and 'catch' use the instruction of '1, 2, 3 Throw'. In this way the face can be 'thrown' and 'caught' around the circle to actors and children until everyone has had a turn and you ask for it to be thrown to you. End the game by letting the face drop. Alternatively you can throw the face to the whole group so that everyone 'catches' it together for a final time and then ask the group to drop the face, rest their hands and give a round of applause.

DEMETRIUS'S FRUSTRATED FACE

Another actor now assumes the frustrated face of Demetrius. This may appear similar to angry, the difference is a subtle one that should be embraced if the children question it. Make sure you can make the distinction yourself between an angry and frustrated face. Once the face is established, an actor on the opposite side of the circle becomes the 'catcher', ready to 'catch' the face of Demetrius.

Slowly say '1, 2, 3 Throw' at the end of which Demetrius 'throws' his face across the circle toward the catcher. Play the game with the whole group exactly as before, ensuring that everyone around the circle has the chance to 'catch' and 'throw' the frustrated face before letting it drop.

HERMIA'S LOVESICK FACE

Another actor now assumes the lovesick face of Hermia. You will have already explored the lovestruck face in earlier games and this gives you the chance to explore the differences. Hermia's lovesick face is softer, like a pining puppy whereas lovestruck is the 'goggle eyed' face of someone whose eyes have been tricked by Puck and has fallen in love at first sight. Once the lovesick face is established, an actor on the opposite side of the circle becomes the catcher, ready to 'catch' the lovesick face of Hermia.

Slowly say '1, 2, 3 Throw' at the end of which Hermia 'throws' her face across the circle toward the catcher. Play the game with the whole group exactly as before, ensuring that everyone around the circle has the chance to 'catch' and 'throw' the lovesick face before letting it drop.

LYSANDER'S THOUGHTFUL FACE

Another actor now assumes the thoughtful face of the final lover, Lysander, his eyes gazing skyward as if distracted by romantic thought. Once the face is established, an actor on the opposite side of the circle becomes the catcher, ready to 'catch' Lysander's thoughtful face.

Slowly say '1, 2, 3 Throw' at the end of which Lysander 'throws' his face across the circle toward the catcher. Play the game with the whole group exactly as before, ensuring that everyone around the circle has the chance to 'catch' and 'throw' the thoughtful face before letting it drop.

The game is over once all four faces have been thrown around the circle and experienced by everybody.

Playing with the children

Play this game with everybody in the circle together. The more committed you are to the faces the more the children will respond. Played correctly your facial muscles should genuinely ache by the end!

Throwing the face, body and voice

This game provides the children with the chance to expand their facial expressiveness through to their bodies and voices within the familiar framework of the game. The lovers' emotional starting points are now extended to encompass a body shape, phrase and voice to be thrown around the circle. These phrases become the beginning of the lovers' narrative.

Throwing the face and body

Demonstration

HELENA

Everyone stands up around the circle, prepared to use their faces and bodies. An actor assumes the jealous face and body shape of Helena, bristling with jealousy from head to toe. A second actor on the opposite side of the room prepares to become the 'catcher'. Once Helena and the catcher are ready, give the instruction of '1, 2, 3 Throw' at which Helena 'throws' her jealous face and body shape across the circle, jumping a little off the ground with the effort, and the catcher 'catches' it, immediately alive and bristling, her whole body 'in a huff', pinched and unhappy.

Use the same instruction of '1, 2, 3 Throw' to play the game with the whole group around the circle, always ensuring that thrower and catcher are ready and making eye contact before they play. Mix the game up so that Helena's jealous face and body is 'thrown' to pairs and small groups and finally to the group as a whole, creating an entire circle of jealous Helenas before finishing back with the original actor.

DEMETRIUS

Everyone remains standing up around the circle and now another actor assumes the frustrated face and body shape of Demetrius, his legs, arms, torso and back quivering with frustrated energy, fists clenched like a boxer. A second actor on the opposite side of the room prepares to become the catcher. Once Demetrius and the catcher are ready, give the instruction of '1, 2, 3 Throw' at which Demetrius 'throws' his frustrated face and body shape across the circle, jumping a little off the ground with the effort, and the catcher 'catches' it, immediately alive with frustrated energy, fists clenched like a boxer, legs, arms, torso and back quivering with dissatisfaction.

Use the same instruction of '1, 2, 3 Throw' to play the game with the whole group around the circle, always ensuring that thrower and catcher are ready and making eye contact before they play. Mix the game up so that the frustrated body of Demetrius is 'thrown' to pairs and small groups and finally to the group as a whole, creating an entire circle of frustrated energy before finishing back with the original actor.

HERMIA

With everyone still standing up around the circle another actor assumes the lovesick face and body shape of Hermia, her body limp, sighing and pining for her love. A second actor on the opposite side of the room prepares to become the catcher. Once Hermia and the catcher are ready, give the instruction of '1, 2, 3 Throw' at which Hermia 'throws' her lovesick face and body shape across the circle, jumping a little off the ground with the effort, and the catcher 'catches' it, immediately floppy and limp, pining like a puppy.

Use the same instruction of '1, 2, 3 Throw' to play the game with the whole group around the circle, always ensuring that thrower and catcher are ready and making eye contact before they play. Vary the game so that the lovesick face and body of Hermia is 'thrown' to pairs and small groups and finally to the group as a whole, creating an entire circle of lovesick, sighing Hermias before finishing back with the original actor.

LYSANDER

With everyone still standing up around the circle a final actor assumes the thoughtful face and body shape of the final lover, Lysander, his body pensive and distracted. A second actor on the opposite side of the room prepares to become the catcher. Once Lysander and the catcher are ready, give the instruction of '1, 2, 3 Throw' at which Lysander 'throws' his thoughtful face and body shape across the circle, jumping a little off the ground with the effort, and the catcher 'catches' it, immediately dreamy and preoccupied, eyes gazing skyward.

As before, use the same instruction of '1, 2, 3 Throw' to play the game with the whole group around the circle, always ensuring that thrower and catcher are ready and making eye contact before they play. Vary the game so that the thoughtful face and body shape of Lysander is 'thrown' to pairs and small groups and finally to the group as a whole, creating an entire circle of thoughtful Lysanders before finishing back with the original actor.

Playing with the children

Keep this stage of the game to the whole circle, encouraging the children to completely embody the transformations through your own total commitment to the lovers' distinctive characteristics. If the children find the game very challenging and need a break from being in the circle, split into pairs or small groups and play. If you play in a pair, you have to give the instruction and simultaneously throw or catch the body at the same time, which is not ideal, but not impossible. Whether playing in pairs or in a large group, the more committed you are to the faces and bodies, the more progress the children are likely to make. Show the children how to play, don't tell them.

Sounds and noises are naturally emitted when playing this game – squeals, grunts and quiet roars emerge innately with the effort of the throw – even when no language is required. Whilst playing, take time to notice whether the children make this natural vocal connection to the 'throw' and 'catch' themselves, as an indicator of how connected their voices are to their physical and emotional life. This will prepare you for the challenge of the next and final stage of the game in which language is added.

Throwing the face, body and voice

Before playing memorize these lines

Helena: We should be woo'd and were not made to woo. I love Demetrius.

Demetrius: I love you not therefore pursue me not. I love Hermia.

Hermia: Lysander and myself shall fly this place, I love Lysander.

Lysander: The path of true love ne'er did run smooth. I love Hermia.

The game is played exactly as before with the addition of language. The characters speak before they throw their body and each catcher speaks once the body shape has been caught.

Lysander and Demetrius's voices should be distinctly different from one another, in tone, accent and register. This becomes crucial for the later game of 'Swords and shadows'. Originally I created Lysander with a French accent and Demetrius as a cockney to give them distinction; choose whatever you like, as long as they are obviously different.

Demonstration

HELENA

Everyone stands up around the circle, prepared to use their faces, bodies and voices. An actor assumes the jealous face and body shape of Helena, bristling with jealousy from head to toe. A second actor on the opposite side of the room prepares to become the catcher. Once Helena and the catcher are ready, give the instruction of '1, 2, 3 Throw' at which Helena speaks;

> We should be woo'd and were not made to woo. I love Demetrius.

She cries the 'oo' sounds as if howling to the moon and immediately 'throws' her jealous face and body shape across the circle, jumping a little off the ground with the effort, and the catcher 'catches' it, immediately alive and bristling, her whole body 'in a huff', pinched and unhappy, repeating Helena's line:

> We should be woo'd and were not made to woo. I love Demetrius.

Use the same instruction of '1, 2, 3 Throw' to play the game with the whole group around the circle, always ensuring that thrower and catcher are ready and making eye contact before they play, speaking the words once they have 'caught' the body. Mix the game up so that Helena's jealous face, body and voice are 'thrown' to pairs and small groups and finally to the group as a whole who speak the line together creating an entire circle of jealous Helenas before finishing back with the original actor.

DEMETRIUS

Another actor assumes the frustrated face and body shape of Demetrius, his legs, arms, torso and back quivering with frustrated energy, fists clenched like a boxer. A second actor on the opposite side of the room prepares to become the catcher. Once Demetrius and the catcher are ready, give the instruction of '1, 2, 3 Throw' at which Demetrius speaks in as distinctive a voice as possible:

> I love you not therefore pursue me not. I love Hermia.

and immediately 'throws' his frustrated face and body shape across the circle, jumping a little off the ground with the effort, and the catcher 'catches' it, alive with frustrated energy, fists clenched like a boxer, legs, arms, torso and back quivering with dissatisfaction and immediately repeating the line:

> I love you not therefore pursue me not. I love Hermia.

Use the same instruction of '1, 2, 3 Throw' to play the game with the whole group around the circle, always ensuring that thrower and catcher are ready and making eye contact before they play, speaking the words once they have 'caught' the body. Mix the game up so that Demetrius's frustrated face, body and voice are 'thrown' to pairs and small groups and finally to the group as a whole who speak the line together creating an entire circle of frustration before finishing back with the original actor.

HERMIA

With everyone still standing up around the circle another actor now assumes the lovesick face and body shape of Hermia, her body limp, sighing and pining for her love. A second actor on the opposite side of the room prepares to become the catcher. Once Hermia and the catcher are ready, give the instruction of '1, 2, 3 Throw' at which Hermia, with a sighing voice, speaks.

> Lysander and myself shall fly this place, I love Lysander.

and immediately 'throws' her lovesick face and body shape across the circle, jumping a little off the ground with the effort, and the catcher 'catches' it, immediately floppy and limp, pining like a puppy, repeating the line:

> Lysander and myself shall fly this place, I love Lysander.

Use the same instruction of '1, 2, 3 Throw' to play the game with the whole group around the circle, always ensuring that thrower and catcher are ready and making eye contact before they play, speaking the words once they have 'caught' the body. Vary the game so that Hermia's lovesick face, body and voice are 'thrown' to pairs and small groups and finally to the group as a whole who speak the line together creating an entire circle of 'lovesick puppies' before finishing back with the original actor.

LYSANDER

Finally another actor assumes the thoughtful face and body shape of Lysander, his body pensive, dreamy and distracted. A second actor on the opposite side of the room prepares to become the catcher. Once Lysander and the catcher are ready, give the instruction of '1, 2, 3 Throw' at which Lysander, with an unforgettable and distinctive tone speaks:

> The path of true love ne'er did run smooth. I love Hermia.

and immediately 'throws' his thoughtful face and body shape across the circle, jumping a little off the ground with the effort, and the catcher 'catches' it, immediately dreamy and preoccupied, eyes gazing skyward, and using the distinctive voice speaks the line:

> The path of true love ne'er did run smooth. I love Hermia.

As before, use the same instruction of '1, 2, 3 Throw' to play the game with the whole group around the circle, ensuring that thrower and catcher are ready and making eye contact before they play. Vary the game so that the thoughtful, dreamy face and body shape of Lysander is 'thrown' to pairs and small groups and finally to the group as a whole, creating an entire circle of thoughtful Lysanders before finishing back with the original actor.

Playing with the children

Choose one of the lovers to concentrate on, or if you feel ambitious you can practise all four, exploring the distinctive differences between them. Experiment with the sporting element of the game, varying the distance between the thrower and catcher to further the children's enjoyment; the greater the distance between them the more effort required to 'throw' and the more preparation required to 'catch'.

Some children instinctively fall over backwards when they are 'catching' as if the force of the face, body and voice is so great it knocks them over. This within reason, is to be encouraged; it is a sure sign there is an imagination at work. It's also fun to play the game with almost no distance between the two players; the diminished effort has the effect of intensifying the emotions, as if the players are 'in close up'.

When you have repeated the game several times, return to the circle to share your game with the group.

Puck's petals

A little western flower
Before milk white, now purple with love's wound
And maidens call it 'love-in-idleness'.

(*A Midsummer Night's Dream*, II, i, 172–4)

Puck squeezes magic juice from the petals of a flower into the eyes of the sleeping lovers, whereby, on waking, they fall in love with the first person they see.

At the beginning of the play, Lysander and Demetrius are in love with Hermia, whilst Helena is in love with Demetrius. Puck's mission is to squeeze the juice into the eyes of Demetrius in order that he should love Helena, but by mistake he squeezes the flower's juice into Lysander's eyes, causing him to fall in love with Helena.

This is a soundless, easy game, exploring the moment Puck squeezes the juice into Lysander's eyes. It allows the children to use their listening silence, (introduced in the game of 'I have had a dream' in Chapter 3) to bring the story to life. The game is short but requires enormous concentration.

Demonstration

Two actors are in the circle, one is Puck, who assumes his mischievous face, and the other is Lysander. Lysander lies down on his back, eyes closed, pretending to be asleep.

Puck takes three rhythmic silent steps toward Lysander, suppressing a mischievous laugh, establishing Puck's sense of mischief. His hands and fingers are in front of him as if holding the magic petals.

He gently holds his hands above Lysander's eyes, about two feet from the ground and rubs his fingertips together as if squeezing juice out of the flower, careful not to wake Lysander. The moment is so quiet that the sound of his fingers can be heard.

With his eyes closed, Lysander listens for the sound of the petals.

When he hears Puck's fingertips he twitches his eyelids, yawns and sighs, creating the POE.

Puck takes three rhythmic silent steps away from Lysander.

The players swap roles and play again.

Playing with the children

Play the game as a group activity, inviting one child at a time to come in to the circle to play Puck while an actor plays Lysander. Encourage the children to use Puck's rhythmic steps, three in and three out to heighten the tension and sense of mischief. You may need to bring an actor into the circle as Puck every so often, either accompanying a child, or taking a turn on their own if the sense of mischief needs re-invigorating. After a few children have had a turn and the game is established, invite the children to play Lysander and continue to play.

If a child feels uncomfortable lying down on the floor as Lysander, he can stand, kneel or crouch, as long as his eyes are closed and visible to Puck. It may be that an actor accompanies the 'sleeping' child and they play Lysander together, the actor encouraging the child to listen as they both wait with their eyes closed for the sound of Puck's petals.

Encourage the group to 'listen to the silence' and watch Lysander's eyes. The aim is to explore the notion of the listening silence for the whole group, wherein the collective sensation is that of heightened attentiveness. As leader, you can enhance this by staying soundless yourself, signalling silently to the children and actors that it's their turn to enter and leave the circle. The game is finished when everyone has had a turn as Puck.

You can split into small groups; playing in groups of three works well so that one adult can support the children. If you have to play in a pair, you may find it necessary to cheat when you are Lysander, peeping through your closed eyes. Once you have repeated the game in your pairs or group, come back to the circle to share.

Adding words

The game can be played with the addition of language.

Demonstration

Before playing memorize this line

Night and Silence, who is here?

Play the game exactly as above. Puck takes his three steps toward Lysander and looking down at him, he whispers:

> Night and Silence, who is here?

The rest of the game remains exactly the same.

Playing with the children

Split into small groups to play and ensure that the children whisper the line, expressing the mischievousness in their voices. As another version, experiment with how the line fits into the rhythm of Puck's three steps, speaking one word per step using:

> Who is here?

Repeat the game a few times and come back to the circle to share.

Lysander's trance

This is a game of eye contact, played by Lysander and Helena in which Lysander's eyes have been tricked; he wakes up, sees Helena and falls in love with her at first sight. This game uses the 'Doyoyoying!' and demands longer periods of eye contact than previously held.

Demonstration

Before playing memorize these lines

Helena: Lysander, if you live, good sir, awake!
Lysander: And run through fire for thy sweet sake
Helena: Say not so.

Two actors are in the circle, an arm's length away from each other, one is Helena, the other Lysander. Lysander's eyes are closed; he is asleep. Helena assumes her jealous expression.
  First, she whispers to Lysander:

> Lysander, awake!

Or

> Lysander, if you live, good sir, awake!

Lysander opens his eyes and making direct eye contact with Helena he immediately makes a 'Doyoyoying!' with his hands, eyes and voice.

Then, keeping full eye contact, and using his distinctive voice he speaks:

> And run through fire for your sweet sake

Helena's expression changes to fearful.

Lysander's eyes are transfixed on Helena's and he maintains the same distance between his and her eyes for the game. She slowly starts to back away and he begins to follow as if she is a magnet pulling him toward her wherever she goes. Their eyes are locked together. Her action is to get away from him but her fear makes her go as slowly as possible.

She is creative with her physical movement, varying its rhythm and trying to 'lose Lysander's eyes' but wherever she goes, he follows.

The movements of their bodies are slow, smooth and trancelike. After a minute or so, Helena places her hands over her eyes, speaking the words 'Say not so', giving the game its POE.

The players take a breathing space, swap roles and play again.

Playing with the children

'Lysander's trance' requires a combination of skills from two fairyland games, the eye contact of 'Lovestruck' and the smooth magnetic physicality of 'Puck's trance'. The key to the trance games is the slow speed and smooth movement with which they are played, encouraging the children to keep their limbs fluid. Initially it's best to try three or four seconds of eye contact rather than push the children to hold it for any longer. This is a game to be played little and often, if you take the children too far from their comfort zone too early, they may very well retreat from trying.

Both characters play this game with different expressions from their introductory faces, Helena's jealous expression turns to fear and Lysander's thoughtfulness disappears in place of lovestruck as a result of Puck's magic. Ensure that the children begin to grasp the idea that 'faces change' by practising the changes as much as they are able, so that they begin to experience how expressions change according to circumstance. Allow the children to swap parts to differentiate between the fearful Helena and the lovestruck Lysander.

If you are feeling adventurous, you can add 'Puck's petals' to the beginning of the game, giving a narrative thread to the story.

When you have repeated the game several times, with or without the addition of 'Puck's petals' come back to the circle to share.

Lovers' trance

To remedy his mistake Puck squeezes the love juice into the eyes of sleeping Demetrius, with whom Helena is in love. Demetrius wakes and declares his love for her, which she believes to be a tormenting joke. Both men, who had previously declared their love for Hermia, are now under the spell of Puck's petals and have been rendered lovestruck for Helena. The three lovers are now inseparably linked together. This game is a more advanced version of 'Puck's trance' and offers a perfect physical representation of the love triangle, allowing a complicated physical relationship to develop between the three lovers. It directly challenges the physical 'stiffness' often associated with autism inviting a flow of movement from one person to the next as well as challenging the children's spatial awareness and encouraging longer periods of concentrated eye focus. The game's inherent expressive power allows the children to communicate physically without ever touching one another.

Demonstration

Three actors are in the circle, playing Helena, Demetrius and Lysander. They introduce themselves, beginning with Helena who assumes a fearful face. Demetrius and Lysander are on either side of her, just an arm's distance away, facing toward her. The two men introduce themselves, both assuming a lovestruck face and then staring at Helena.

To play, Helena looks to Demetrius who makes a' Doyoyoying!' with his hands, eyes and voice. Helena raises the palm of her hand to Demetrius's face as if to stop him. She leaves it there, one hand's width distance away. She then looks to Lysander who also makes a 'Doyoyoying!' with his hands, eyes and voice. Helena raises her other hand up, her palm to his face as if to stop him. Helena now has both hands raised, palms toward the two lovers' faces.

Helena slowly begins to move her hands and her body and the two men follow her around the circle, keeping their eyes fixed to her palms, maintaining an equal distance from her hands at all times. They are magnetically pushed and pulled by her every move, all three players keeping the movements slow, soft and flexible, almost dreamlike. It is as if they are her puppets: she may move one up whilst she moves the other down, one in front whilst the other is behind, alternating them both over and under each other's bodies. There is no end to the twisting and turning she experiments with, now she has them in her physical power.

After a few minutes of play, Helena gently claps her hands and the players swap roles, assuming the appropriate expression depending on which part they are playing. They play the game in silence, finishing when all three actors have had a turn at playing each part.

Playing with the children

Encourage the children to discover new ways to move their bodies in relation to each player. Your own use of smooth flowing movement will be a starting point for the children to copy but they may need encouragement to alter their natural body movements; adjusting from sharp and stiff to soft and flexible. They may have never moved their bodies in this smooth way before, in which case progress may be slow and the changes in their movements almost imperceptible; you need to watch carefully for all signs of improvement and let them know when you see it, what seems small to you may well be monumental for the child.

All the advice for 'Puck's trance' is applicable for this game; it needs to be played as slowly and quietly as possible so that a physical language can be established between the players. Make sure that the leader (Helena) is watching her two followers (Lysander and Demetrius) and caring for them all the time; the children sometimes watch their own hands when they lead, which can block their flow of movement. Encourage the leaders to move their hands and keep their eyes on their followers, it will teach you a lot about the child if they find this difficult or impossible. Put succinctly, the leader should watch the followers' bodies, the followers watch the leader's hands.

Depending on numbers in the group, play with them as part of a three, giving encouragement where needed or let three children play together while you stay close, moving with them round the room, offering support and guidance.

Again, you can add 'Puck's petals' to the beginning of this game, squeezing the juice into the eyes of Demetrius and Lysander to enhance the narrative of the story. Take this opportunity to highlight the connection between 'Puck's petals' and 'Lovers' trance', allowing the children to appreciate narrative and consequence; it is *because* of Puck's petals that the lovers are in the trance.

When you have repeated the game several times, with or without the addition of 'Puck's petals' come back to the circle to share.

Chapter 6

Darkness of night

Never so weary, never so in woe,
Bedabbl'd with the dew and torn with briars
I can no further crawl, no further go,
My legs can keep no pace with my desires.
(*A Midsummer Night's Dream*, III, ii, 471–4)

Demetrius and Lysander, their eyes tricked by the juice of Puck's petals fight each other for Helena's love, travelling deeper into the forest, until enveloped in the darkness of night they are unable to see. Puck leads all four lovers through the darkness to a clearing for sleep.

These games are physically challenging and involve increased interaction with others in order to play. By the time you tackle these complicated games you will have begun to develop your own ways of playing, using prompting and instructive playfulness and you should also have a good understanding of the needs of the children you work with. It would be unrewarding for you and the children to play the games in this chapter without working through most of the earlier games in the book.

The games

- Invisible swords
- Swords and shadows
- Follow my voice
- Waking up

The characters

- Helena
- Hermia
- Lysander
- Demetrius
- Puck

The targets

- Improving spatial awareness
- Improving speech and language skills
- Developing sensory awareness
- Playing a part and playing with others

Invisible swords

Demetrius and Lysander, both lovestruck for Helena, now begin to fight over her. This is a simple sword-fighting game adapted to challenge the children's spatial awareness and physical co-ordination. Once the physical game has been mastered, text is added providing further challenges for the children's speech and language.

Demonstration

Two actors are in the circle, playing Lysander and Demetrius, they stand about five or six feet apart, maintaining this distance between each other for the whole game and never making any physical contact. They introduce themselves, both assuming a frustrated face and then making eye contact with each other. Next they stretch their arms out in front of their bodies, hands clasped together as if holding an invisible double-handed sword, knees slightly bent, preparing to spring into action. They come back to this position each time they begin. To play they take turns as striker and receiver. (There is enough room for the striker to swing her invisible sword in front of her body without touching the receiver.)

Maintaining their distance, the striker swings her invisible sword from right to left aiming toward the receiver's head. The receiver ducks down and pops back up in response to the strike as if the sword has gone over her body. The striker waits for them both to settle, takes the starting position and makes eye contact with the receiver before the next swing.

Next the striker takes a second swing from right to left aiming toward the receiver's feet, and the receiver responds by jumping up as if dodging the sword. She jumps as high as she can, knees bent up underneath her. After this, both players take time to settle again, take the starting position and make eye contact.

Finally the striker makes a stab with her invisible sword toward the receiver's tummy and the receiver responds with a leap backward to dodge the tummy blow. This is the end of the first round. There are always three strikes in this order for one player's turn.

Now the actors swap roles, the receiver becomes the striker, the striker the receiver and they repeat the exercise. The actors swap round three times in order for the children to learn the game. The leader describes what is happening during the demonstration.

A variation of the game is for the striker to strike the head, feet or tummy in any order she chooses, which requires a higher level of concentration from both players. This unknown quality increases the game's excitement; there is nothing to stop the striker making three swings exclusively to the feet, head or tummy and the receiver will then be able to 'get her own back' when they swap roles. Played in this way the settling moment of eye contact between each strike becomes crucial.

Playing with the children

This exercise can highlight common difficulties for the children beyond those of physical co-ordination. Taking turns, taking initiative and understanding the difference between action and response are all skills necessary for the game, all of which the children may struggle with. If you swing your invisible sword toward their head, they may not duck down, but simply swing theirs back at you and however hard you try to explain that its their turn to duck they will continue to mirror your movements. It can be very frustrating for everyone involved and especially confusing for the child who would like to play the game if they could.

Do not continue if it's clear you're not getting anywhere. The famous definition of madness being to 'repeat the same instruction whilst expecting a different result' is a useful one to remember and act upon. If something really doesn't work, neither you nor the child is at fault, it means you may be using the wrong approach and you should change your strategy.

As ever, your ultimate aim is for the children to experience what the game *feels* like. To do this, play one role at a time together, creating a 'striker duo' and then a 'receiver duo'. Begin by being the striker with the child; teach her how to strike her invisible sword by physically guiding her arms and hands and doing it with her. Do not stand in front, but join her from behind, as if you were teaching her how to use a golf club. Make your practice as rhythmic, fun and forceful as possible.

After some repetition, enlist another child or adult to be the receiver. Encourage the child as your 'striker partner' to make eye contact as much as possible with the receiver whilst you play as a duo. Concentrate solely on your role as 'striker partner', never allowing the child to struggle with initiative but rather to succeed in playing the game, thanks to your support. You may feel this is enough to share, in which case come back to the circle and when it's your turn, come into the circle as a duo and enlist someone to be the receiver to your striker partnership.

When you teach this child the receiver's role, use exactly the same approach. Become a 'receiver duo' and practise the duck, jump and leap before you enlist a striker to play with you. Come back to the circle, enlist someone to be the striker and share your 'receiver duo' with the group. Play this way until you feel that the game is embedded in the child's body and then experiment little by little in removing your support and seeing if she can take the initiative for striking and receiving by herself.

For children who find this game relatively easy, encourage them to utilize their physical energy, bringing the lovers' frustration to life. As long as there is enough space around you to play and an appropriate distance between the two players, the swing from the striker should be as forceful as possible, employing their full body weight and power to swing the invisible sword. It's fun to imagine that the sword is very heavy and takes huge physical effort to hold, let alone swing. For the receiver they should be responding with as much energy as they can, ducking very low, jumping very high and leaping back as far as they can.

When the children try the next level of the game, where the receiver doesn't know which strike is coming next, ensure they make good use of eye contact and encourage the children to try to 'read' each other's bodies, anticipating what's about to happen allowing them to heighten their physical experience of living. Rather like a tennis match, the moments of silence between the strikes should be filled with eye contact and anticipation from both players, similar to the still quiet moments before a great shot.

When you have repeated the game several times, come back to the circle to share.

Adding words

The game remains exactly the same with the addition of text for both players.

Demonstration

Before playing memorize these lines

Lysander:	I say I love her more
Demetrius:	If thou say so, withdraw!
Lysander	Now follow if you dare
Demetrius:	Follow? I'll go with you

Two actors are in the circle, five or six feet apart, playing Lysander and Demetrius.

As before, they prepare to play the game; ready with their invisible double-handed swords, knees slightly bent, preparing to spring into action. For this demonstration the striker uses the original order; first head, then feet and then tummy and the receiver responds accordingly with ducking, jumping and leaping back. The first striker is Lysander who speaks the first line, using the natural rhythm by which the words and the 'strikes of the sword' fit together, in bold type here for guidance.

I **say** I **love** her **more**

He makes his three strikes and Demetrius responds accordingly, ducking, hopping and leaping back. Next Demetrius makes his three strikes, speaking his line:

If **thou** say **so**, with**draw!**

and Lysander ducks, jumps and leaps back accordingly.

Lysander takes the next three strikes speaking his next line:

Now **follow if** you **dare**

and Demetrius responds. Finally Demetrius becomes the striker and says his last line:

Follow? I'll **go** with **you.**

with Lysander responding as the receiver. The actors emphasize the frustration of the lovers through their faces, voices, bodies and movements. After a little breathing space, the players swap roles and play again.

Playing with the children

You can modify the script if the addition of the language proves too much of a challenge; using a simpler version the children can still face the test of adding language but without the relative complexity of this text. The simplest version is to have Lysander say 'No, No, No' when he is the striker, speaking one word on each strike and for Demetrius to say 'Yes, Yes, Yes' when he is the striker. The game stays exactly the same.

A moderate version is to take either the first two lines:

Lysander: I say I love her more.
Demetrius   If thou say so, withdraw!

Or the second two lines

Lysander: Now follow if you dare.
Demetrius: Follow? I'll go with you.

and repeat them until they feel easy and natural.

If you are feeling adventurous you can play the harder version of the game where the striker chooses the order of her strikes thereby keeping the receiver more alert, whilst speaking the lines at the same time.

Once a comfortable level of language has been introduced and repeated, come back to the circle to share.

Swords and shadows

When I come where he calls, then he's gone.

(*A Midsummer Night's Dream*, III, ii, 141)

Lysander and Demetrius, still determined to fight each other, travel deeper into the forest, until they are enveloped in the darkness of night and are unable to see. Puck is invisible to them and takes advantage of their 'blindness' with further teasing. He imitates their voices, making them think they are following each other whilst in fact they are following him and becoming increasingly lost.

This is the most complex game so far, developing the demands of spatial awareness and language skills. Essentially it is a combination of the 'Shadow' game and 'Invisible swords' with new text and a physical free rein thrown into the mix. The first demonstration shows Lysander and Puck and the second demonstration adds Demetrius.

Demonstration

Before playing memorize these lines

Lysander: Where art thou proud Demetrius?
Puck: Here villain, drawn and ready, where art thou?

Two actors are in the circle, playing Puck and Lysander. Puck is standing directly behind Lysander, an arm's distance away, as if ready to play the 'Shadow' game. Lysander makes his introduction:

I'm Lysander and I'm looking for Demetrius

He assumes the starting position for 'Invisible swords', knees slightly bent, arms stretched out in front of him and hands clasped together holding his double-handed sword. He introduces a new facial expression – 'searching' as if he is trying to see through the thick darkness.

He speaks his line with his distinctive voice:

Where art thou proud Demetrius?

Puck makes his introduction:

I'm Puck and I'm pretending to be Demetrius using my voice.

He assumes his mischievous face and body and, staying hidden behind Lysander, he speaks his line to tease him, imitating the distinctive voice of Demetrius.

Here villain, drawn and ready, where art thou?

Lysander hears the voice, and keeping his arms stretched out in front of him he swings round a full circle on the spot as if to chop off Demetrius's head behind him. Puck ducks down to avoid the blow and Lysander swipes only the air,;Puck pops up again when Lysander gets back to where he was. Puck is delighted with his mischief and Lysander is totally confused. (This shared movement is nicknamed the 'swing and duck down'.)

Lysander begins to walk around the circle, searching more eagerly for Demetrius, meanwhile Puck follows behind him, shadowing his every move. Lysander adds fearful to his searching expression, his arms stretched out in front of him, hands still clasping the sword.

A few moments later he stops again and calls out his line

Where art thou proud Demetrius?

Puck is directly behind him and repeats his line, again imitating the voice of Demetrius:

Here villain, drawn and ready, where art thou?

Lysander and Puck repeat the 'swing and duck down'. Immediately after, the two of them proceed to move slowly around the circle, as if in a darkened forest, Puck shadowing Lysander. As they move, they repeat their two lines, which are punctuated each time by the 'swing and duck down' movement. They repeat the sequence three more times, each 'swing and duck down' providing a little POE, and as the game proceeds, Puck becomes more mischievous and Lysander becomes increasingly confused, resulting in the game becoming increasingly fast and heightened in emotion.

Playing with the children

Practise the 'swing and duck down' movement on its own to begin with using whatever teaching strategies you need depending on the cognition and ability of the children, eliciting the help of another adult if you need to pair up as a duo. When playing Puck in this game, many children will have the instinct to duck down but their bodies will not obey their mind's impulse. I taught one boy in particular, who tried so hard to stay on the spot and duck straight down, but however hard he tried his feet kept moving him sideways. He would then look around after he had moved to check whether he had done it right, as if he had no idea where his body had taken him. To practise, an actor spoke the lines from the side of the circle, allowing the boy to concentrate solely on the movement, which he tried with every fibre of his being to get right. He never totally mastered it, but was elated and transformed by the experience of trying. You are not seeking perfection with these games; it is in the act of trying something new that the intervention is at its most beneficial.

If the children struggle with the free rein element of the game, establish a good steady rhythm for the two players as they move around the circle – three strong steps then stop and speak – this is simple to repeat and will make it easier for them to increase speed when they are more confident. In addition to this, encourage the children to explore Lysander's 'blindness', it's interesting and enjoyable for them to pretend they can't see whilst keeping their eyes open.

Feel free to explore the whole sequence with no text, the physicality of the game is a language in itself, a silent narrative; therefore allow the children to express themselves physically in as animated a way as possible. The only text you need for the game to work is for Puck to say 'Ready!' which stimulates the swing movement from Lysander. The rest can be played silently allowing the children to engage fully with the physical demands of the game. The addition of words should not be a burden, but rather another means of expressing feelings and intentions once the game is embedded in the children's bodies. When you have repeated the game several times, come back to the circle to share.

Adding Demetrius

The addition of Demetrius stretches Puck's vocal skills as he must now imitate the distinct voices of both the men, making a clear difference between the two. Meanwhile progressing from two to three characters increases the challenge of spatial awareness for all three players, intensifying their concentrated turn-taking.

Demonstration

Before playing memorize this line

Demetrius: Thou runaway, thou coward, art thou fled?

Three actors are in the circle, playing Puck, Lysander and Demetrius. Puck and Lysander begin exactly as before, they make their introductions and begin to move around the circle, Puck shadowing Lysander. They speak their lines as before and make one 'swing and duck down'. Demetrius now joins the circle as far away from Lysander as possible. While he speaks Lysander makes small movements around the circle, searching in the dark for his enemy. Demetrius makes his introduction:

I'm Demetrius and I'm looking for Lysander

He then assumes the same physical position as Lysander, ready to play 'Invisible swords', knees slightly bent, arms stretched out in front of him and hands clasped together holding his double-handed sword. His face is 'searching' as if he can't see through the thick darkness.

With frustration, in his distinctive voice he speaks his line:

Thou runaway, thou coward, art thou fled?

Puck hears Demetrius and moves across to stand behind him. Imitating Lysander's voice, Puck speaks:

Here villain, drawn and ready, where art thou?

Now Demetrius swings round and Puck ducks down and pops up again, completing the 'swing and duck down' movement.

Demetrius sets off around the circle as does Lysander, both are searching for the other and move slowly as if in the dark, taking care not to get too close to each other.

One full round with all three actors goes like this.

Lysander:	Where art thou proud Demetrius?
Puck:	*(shadowing Lysander, imitating Demetrius's voice)*
	Here villain, drawn and ready, where art thou?
	(Lysander and Puck complete the 'swing and duck down' movement)
	(Lysander continues to walk, Puck shadowing him)
Demetrius:	Thou runaway, thou coward, art thou fled?
Puck:	*(shadowing Demetrius, imitating Lysander's voice)*
	Here villain, drawn and ready, where art thou?
	(Demetrius and Puck complete the 'swing and duck down' movement.

When Puck feels the game is up, he leaves the circle at which point Lysander and Demetrius take a deep breath and together speak the final words, providing the POE:

Demetrius and Lysander: He is gone!

Playing with the children

If the children are able to handle both language and movement at the same time there is a lot of fun to be had with the imitation of the two lovers' voices. You should already have established that Lysander and Demetrius have very different voices, which can be created with instantly recognizable accents, tones and register. Encourage the children to explore how distinct they can make these differences, using whatever inspiration they choose; imaginative, familiar or cartoon. If they are unable to create the voices be prepared to do so yourself and either speak for the children or in unison with them; you will very likely have to use your prompting skills in this game. Once Lysander and Demetrius are speaking with unique voices, ensure that Puck is able to imitate them both. Additionally the lovers must keep the fearful, searching expression in their faces and allow that to affect their voice.

At its best this game flows with a non-stop physical energy and all three players take initiative for their movements around the circle.

Using instructive playfulness and prompting, support the children and give them what they need to bring the scene to life; you may need to physically guide them in order for them to experience how the game feels or you may need to move between all three children to prompt them with their lines. Or both. You can also prompt from the side, as long as it's clear whom you are prompting.

When you have repeated the game several times, come back to the circle to share.

Follow my voice

Still under the spell of Puck, the four exhausted lovers are led through the dark forest by the sound of Puck's voice. The game explores this final part of the lovers' journey, as they keep their eyes closed and follow Puck's sound, seeing with their ears.

The purpose of 'Follow my voice' is to increase sensory awareness. The game stretches the boundaries of trust and gives the children new levels of responsibility in terms of caring for each other whilst playing. One player is in control and the other has their eyes closed, allowing themselves to be led. It is a classic drama game adapted to support the narrative of the play while simultaneously offering the children a new, challenging sensory experience.

There are two versions of this game, the first played in pairs and the second as a whole group activity.

Demonstration

Before playing memorize these lines. (Initially Puck uses simple sounds but he can also use these phrases to play.)

> Follow me
> Ho Ho Ho
> Come hither, I am here

And for the adventurous:

> Yet but three? come one more, two of both kinds make up four

Two actors are in the circle, one plays Puck, while the other chooses which of the lovers to play for this demonstration I choose Helena. They introduce themselves and assume their expressions; Puck is mischievous whilst the lover assumes an exhausted expression with face and body shape. They stand face to face in the circle, about three paces away from each other. Puck creates a sound with which to lead Helena. The sound can be a whistle, a coo, a boom, a trill, anything that he enjoys making with his voice, it should be short, repeatable and instantly recognizable.

He makes the sound once so that Helena knows what to listen for and then Helena closes her eyes. Puck waits a few seconds and then makes the sound again. Helena hears the sound and takes one step toward it, keeping her hands and arms by her sides when she moves. Puck quietly moves to a different point in the circle, stands still and once more makes the sound. Helena changes direction and takes a step toward the sound, keeping her eyes closed and her hands and arms by her sides.

The game continues in this way with Puck changing direction and moving as silently as possible around the circle while Helena, keeping her eyes closed, intently listens for the next sound and takes one step toward it each time it comes. After a minute or two Puck leads Helena toward him with his sound and when she is within touching distance he gently blows air onto Helena's forehead as if to wake her from the spell. Alternatively he can say 'Awake'. They take a breathing space, swap roles and begin again.

Playing with the children

Some children find it very difficult to keep their eyes closed; to be voluntarily led in the dark involves a relinquishing of control, which for children whose anxiety levels may be high requires a considerable leap of faith. For these children the game can be very short, just one sound from Puck, one step from the lover and then a rest with eyes open again. If the child places their hands over their eyes it demonstrates a real understanding of the game but I do not recommend placing your hands over a child's eyes unless they expressly ask you to do so.

If necessary you can pair up with an anxious child and 'go blind' together, enlisting another adult or capable child to lead you both. In this case you should take the leap of faith yourself, close your eyes and hold hands with the child, or cuddle them in some way so you can move together, listening out for the sound and taking your steps toward it as a pair, encouraging the child as you make your progress. If the child opens their eyes, your enlisted adult can stop the game for a rest and only then should you open yours – your demonstration of faith will act as an example for the child.

When the child leads, your instructive playfulness is very useful, as you may well have to encourage them to make the sound in order for you to take a step toward them whilst keeping your eyes closed; it makes for an amusing version but initially it may be the only way to play.

If the child has the cognition to understand the game, encourage them to keep their hands and arms as still as possible, thereby heightening their physical experience. Be sure to remind them of the story and ask them to choose which lover they would like to play, ensuring that their characterization of Puck's mischievousness and the lover's exhaustion remains enjoyable. You can add the original characteristic of the lover to their exhausted state, exploring how an exhausted but jealous Helena moves around the circle. The same combinations apply for the other three; the exhausted, frustrated Demetrius, the exhausted, lovesick Hermia and the exhausted, thoughtful Lysander are all fun to play, encouraging further exploration of faces and feelings.

When you have repeated the game several times, come back to the circle to share.

Playing as a group

Demonstration

This demonstration is not in the circle. Ideally five actors will demonstrate, beginning at one end of the room with the children watching from the other side. One actor is Puck and the remaining four play the lovers. They each assume the lovers' original characteristics, adding in the exhausted expression. (If there are fewer actors to demonstrate, simply have fewer lovers.) They stand at least one pace apart in a staggered line and Puck stands opposite them about three paces away. Puck demonstrates his sound and the actors all close their eyes.

To begin, Puck makes his sound and the lovers take one step toward it. They need to take care not to bump into each other and in this version they use their hands and arms in front and around themselves to help their spatial awareness. If they do touch one another, they adjust themselves to find a clear space. After each step Puck allows them to settle, establishing the listening silence and then makes his sound again. Once more the four lovers take one step toward it, adjusting themselves accordingly to be in their own space.

Puck and the lovers continue their journey across the room, each lover becoming increasingly exhausted with each sound and step, they can be crawling by the end. Finally Puck leads them close to him and blows air onto each of their foreheads to 'wake them up'. Alternatively he whispers 'Awake' to each one.

Playing with the children

This version remains a group activity. One child plays Puck and the rest of the children join the actors as the lovers. As leader, remain open-eyed and in charge of the game, encouraging and supporting actors and children if they need it, whilst silently communicating with the child playing Puck. The group position themselves at one end of the room, choosing which lover to play and assuming the specific characteristics. If a child needs assistance then an actor can pair up, holding hands or physically supporting them as they move forward.

Puck then demonstrates his sound and the group of lovers close their eyes. The room should be completely silent, encourage the children to absorb the silence thereby heightening their sense of hearing. Puck begins by making his specific sound and the whole group takes one step toward it, using their hands and arms to feel their way forward, spreading out if they need to find more space. They then wait, attentive, listening for the next sound. Puck waits for them to settle and for the listening silence in the room to become palpable. He then makes his sound again and the group takes another step toward him, repeating the heightened, attentive experience once more. In this way the child playing Puck is in control of the whole group, leading them all around the room, with support and encouragement from the leader if necessary.

To finish the game Puck blows air onto the foreheads of the lovers, alternatively he whispers 'Awake' at which point everybody opens their eyes and the game is over. Another child can now have a turn at playing Puck. It's also possible to have two or three Pucks working as a team leading the group around the circle and taking it in turns to make the sound. The game must always be played slowly, with a short settling period before each sound for everyone to experience the listening silence. This group version of the game is complete when each child has had a turn as Puck.

Waking up

> Methinks I see things with parted eye
> When everything seems double
> > (*A Midsummer Night's Dream*, IV, i, 196–7)

At the end of the story Puck squeezes a remedy into Lysander's eyes causing him to fall in love with Hermia once more, creating a happy ending for them all.

This game uses a combination of the heartbeat rhythm, eye contact and the sense of touch to provide an expressive transformation from sadness to happiness.

Demonstration

Before playing memorize these lines

Puck:	I'll apply
	To your eye
	Gentle Lover, remedy
Hermia:	Are you sure we are awake?
Hermia/Lysander:	We are awake!

Three actors are in the circle, they play Hermia, Lysander and Puck. Hermia and Lysander sit back to back on the floor in the middle of the circle. They close their eyes and assume troubled, sad expressions as if they are dreaming bad dreams. They place their hands on their hearts. Puck stands a few paces away from them, he assumes a worried face and places his hand on his heart.

To begin all three players start to make their heartbeats, Hermia and Lysander make a strong, slow and sad rhythm whilst Puck's heartbeat rhythm is twice as fast, as if his heart is racing with panic. He begins to move quickly around the pair watching them. Hermia and Lysander keep their eyes closed, all three players maintain their specific heartbeat rhythms throughout this first stage.

After a few seconds Puck speaks:

> I'll apply
> To your eye
> Gentle Lover, remedy

Puck rubs his fingers toward Lysander's eyes and Lysander moves his face in response. Hermia and Lysander both sigh and yawn but do not wake. They continue with their sleepy heartbeats.

Puck continues to circle them. He repeats the lines:

> I'll apply
> To your eye
> Gentle Lover, remedy

Again, Puck rubs his fingers toward Lysander's eyes and Lysander moves his face in response. Hermia and Lysander both sigh and yawn but do not wake. They continue with their sleepy heartbeats, maintaining their sad expressions.

Puck continues to circle them. Finally he speaks again, emphasizing the final word:

> I'll apply
> To your eye
> Gentle Lover, remedy

This time the two lovers open their eyes. They drop their hands. Puck changes the rhythm of his heartbeat from speedy to slow as if adopting the loving rhythm of a remedy. This is the only sound to be heard, Puck continues it until the lovers begin to speak.

During Puck's slow heartbeat Hermia and Lysander slowly begin to turn their bodies around toward each other, allowing their expressions of sadness and frustration to melt away. When they are facing each other they slowly lift their faces up so that they begin to find each other's eyes. When they make eye contact they hold it for as long as possible and begin to smile. Hermia speaks:

> Are you sure we are awake?

They raise their hands up to make contact palm to palm. They break into large smiles. Together they both speak:

> We *are* awake!

As they speak these last words Puck finishes his slow heartbeats.

After some breathing space the actors swap roles and demonstrate again.

Playing with the children

The heart of the game is at the end, when the characters' expressions change from sad and frustrated to loving and peaceful. If the children are struggling with the words play a silent version. Two players simply sit back to back making sad expressions and heartbeats. They slowly turn round to face each other and change their faces and heartbeats to express love. This moment often results in laughter, which should always be encouraged.

Use 'Puck's petals' within the game for the moment of the remedy and ensure that Lysander and Hermia respond to this moment each time it is repeated. Encourage the children to fully experience the expressive facial transformation from the beginning of the game – eyes closed, sad sleepy faces and thumping heartbeats to the opposing sensations at the end of the game – full eye contact, peaceful smiles and palms touching.

When the children have repeated the game and swapped roles come back to the circle to share.

Part II

The Tempest

Boy: It's not logical
Me: You're right, it's not logical, it's magic

Columbus Ohio. 2014

The play is set on an island inhabited by two creatures, Caliban and Ariel who together embody the four elements of nature. The spirit Ariel is made of fire and air whilst the earth-bound Caliban, a monster described as half man half fish, is created of earth and water. Before the arrival of Prospero and his daughter Miranda, these two creatures had been the sole inhabitants of the island: Ariel trapped in a cloven pine by the cruel witch Sycorax and Caliban, the freckled whelp son of Sycorax, seemingly left to live there on his own. Sycorax makes no appearance in the play.

Twelve years before the play begins, Prospero the banished duke of Milan and his young daughter Miranda, landed on the island's shores. Prospero made Caliban his slave and for the duration of the play they embody a master/slave relationship, in argument over whom the island belongs to. Prospero used his magic to free Ariel from her pine tree for which he made her his servant, promising her liberty once his demands are done.

Chapter 7

Caliban

When thou cam'st first
Thou strok'st me and made much of me
(The Tempest, I, ii, 397–9)

These first games use Caliban as a focus for the children. The games explore his relationship to Prospero, Ariel and Miranda, revealing a different facet of his personality for each.

Characters

- Caliban
- Prospero
- Ariel
- Miranda

Games

- Throwing the face
- Cramps
- Four 'Shadow' games
- Sounds and shadows
- Toads, beetles, bats
- Teaching Caliban to speak
- Hello, too close, goodbye
- Gibberish

Targets

- Facial expressiveness
- Role-play
- Taking turns
- Spatial awareness
- Vocal awareness
- Keeping physical boundaries

Begin every session with a 'Hello heartbeat' circle, exactly as described in Part I. Follow this with 'Throwing the Face', which is described here to introduce the central character of Caliban.

Throwing the face

Caliban's prime emotion is one of anger toward Prospero, who has taken away his liberty and made the island his own. 'Throwing the face' introduces the children to Caliban, connecting his character to the primary sensation of anger and injustice. The game allows the children to explore and express their own anger for a few seconds at a time within the safe, playful setting of the game.

Demonstration

Immediately after the 'Hello heartbeats' with everyone still sitting around the circle, an actor assumes the angry face of Caliban. The face is energized and frowning, the anger actively affecting his upper body and voice, with clenched fists and a rumbling growl. Once the face is established, an actor on the opposite side of the circle becomes the 'catcher', ready to 'catch' the face of Caliban.

Slowly say '1, 2, 3 Throw' at the end of which Caliban 'throws' his face toward the catcher. The action from Caliban is as if a mask is being flung from his face, requiring physical and vocal effort. The 'catcher' immediately assumes Caliban's angry face with an element of surprise as if it has landed from nowhere. He keeps the face energized, with fists clenched and a low growl until you instruct him to throw it again.

Now choose another actor or child to be the 'catcher' and instruct the new Caliban to get ready to throw the face. When both players are ready use the instruction of '1, 2, 3 Throw'. In this way the face can be 'thrown' and 'caught' around the circle to actors and children until everyone has had a turn and you ask for it to be thrown to you. To end the game throw the face to the whole group so that everyone 'catches' it together for a final time and then ask the group to drop the face, rest their hands and give a round of applause.

If you are demonstrating alone, use picture cards to introduce the angry face of Caliban, make the face yourself and 'throw' it to the most able child in the circle. From there, slowly teach and play the game, using yourself as the thrower and the catcher as often as you need.

Playing with the children

Play the game as a group sitting around the circle. The key to this game is the speed with which the anger is 'caught' and 'thrown', creating lightning-fast changes across the features of the face and allowing a cathartic experience of anger to be deeply felt for its short duration, but then immediately erased and forgotten once it has been 'thrown away'. Be careful that in the interest of speed you do not erase the chance for the children to experience the anger; create the feeling that time stops and that the child has a boundless opportunity to explore and embody the angry sensations before throwing them to the next person.

Some children may refuse the anger, burying their faces in their hands. Do not push them too hard to play with you – fruitless encouragement will result in nothing but frustration for you all. If after a couple of attempts it's clear that the child will be distressed by playing, you should let them pass, continue to play with the rest of the group and always offer them the opportunity to join. They will be grateful for the respect you have shown their feelings and much more likely to try to play in the future.

Adding words

Demonstration

Before playing memorize these words

Caliban: This island's mine
        by Sycorax my mother
        Which you took from me.

Play 'Throwing the face' exactly as before, one actor assuming Caliban's angry face, with fists clenched and growling. Before you give the instruction to throw, tell the group that they are going to find out what Caliban says and why he is so angry. Give the instruction '1, 2, 3 Throw'.

Using all his anger and force Caliban speaks the first line:

> This island's mine

elongating the last vowel sound in the word 'mine', creating a long 'aahhh'. He then throws the face across the room to the 'catcher' who immediately assumes the angry face, with clenched fists and growling voice. He takes a breath and repeats the words:

> This island's mine

Now choose another actor or child to be the 'catcher' and when both players are ready to 'throw' and 'catch' use the instruction of '1, 2, 3 Throw'. In this way Caliban's angry face and voice are 'thrown' and 'caught' around the circle. If the children are confident with their language skills, add the next lines one by one, so that finally the full phrase:

> This island's mine, by Sycorax my mother
> Which you took from me.

is being 'thrown' and 'caught' around the circle.

Playing with the children

Remain sitting on the floor, playing as a group around the circle. Remember that this initial game of 'Throwing the face' serves as a bridge toward acting, and should create a desire in the children to be on their feet to play. As the game intensifies with more of the lines being learnt and the emotional quality of anger becoming heightened, you can sit up on your knees allowing more physical engagement, even beating your fists on the ground as you speak, but resisting the temptation to stand.

When expressing anger in this game, or any of the emotions during any of the games in the book, do not raise your voice or shout. It is likely that very loud voices will be painful for the children as indeed they are for anyone. It is completely possible to explore an entire, rich landscape of emotions without ever raising your voice – it is emotional engagement that counts.

When demonstrating and playing with the children experiment with turning the volume of your voice down in relation to your emotions and encourage the children to do the same – the more intense the emotion the quieter your voice. This immediately adds dramatic tension, creating the effect of danger and excitement whilst remaining in a safe playful environment. When the face and voice have been thrown and caught around the circle, and Caliban's sense of injustice is embedded within the group, you will be ready to explore his character further, up on your feet for the next games.

Cramps

Prospero uses his magic to wield tortuous power over Caliban creating a classic servant/master relationship out of which neither character can escape.

Cramps develops this servant/master bond into one of monster/wizard providing a vein of fantasy and humour which underpins the threatening element of the story. Role-playing, turn-taking and a heightened sensory awareness are all embedded within this game.

Demonstration

Before playing memorize these lines

Prospero: Cramps
          Better
Caliban: This island's mine

Two actors stand facing each other in the circle a few feet away from each other. The first is Caliban who assumes the low, curved shape of a monster. He can be as unruly as he chooses to be with knees bent and his face contorted with anger. The other actor is Prospero, upright, ostensibly calmer and more in control. His facial expression is commanding. They maintain these physical lives whilst making no physical contact throughout the whole game.

To begin they circle each other, Caliban increasingly frustrated like a caged animal and Prospero increasingly self-righteous and arrogant. After a few seconds Prospero points to Caliban, clicks his fingers and says:

Cramps

At this, Caliban immediately clutches his sides as if overwhelmed by cramps and collapses on the floor under Prospero's spell. Writhing on the floor Caliban cries out:

This island's mine

He remains under the spell of Prospero and continues to 'have cramps' repeating his phrase as many times as he chooses, whilst Prospero silently delights in his own petty authority. They make no physical contact. After about ten seconds or so Prospero claps his hands saying:

Better

At which point the 'spell is magically broken' and the cramps immediately disappear, allowing Caliban to recover himself, get back to his feet and assume his body shape, contorted with anger and fearful of Prospero's next 'spell'. This marks the end of one turn of the game.

Prospero remains in control, they continue circling each other and after a few seconds they repeat the whole sequence twice more, beginning each time with Prospero pointing to Caliban, clicking his fingers and giving him the cramps and ending with Prospero clapping his hands saying 'Better'.

Once the players have played three times, they take a breathing space, swap roles and play again, the master becoming the slave and the slave now having 'revenge' on the master.

Playing with the children

I have never met a child who didn't like this game. To have ultimate power over another person at the click of your fingers is enjoyable but the children's pleasure in pretending to be in pain, writhing on the floor in agony as poor Caliban is often a revelation. Ensure that you are fully committed to the game every time you play, offering the children whatever help they need depending on their cognition.

Begin by asking the child which part they would like to play first saying, 'monster or wizard?' These generic names are important as they reinforce the images in the mind's eye, and are especially useful when helping the child assume the character's initial physical life.

The POE lies in the moment Caliban receives the cramps and falls to the floor; however, there is a state of heightened awareness that should be fully explored by both players in the moments just before Prospero gives Caliban the cramps. In these moments Prospero has all the power and Caliban's senses are intensified by the inevitable 'agony' that he knows is coming. This creates an intimate, listening silence with both players soundlessly 'reading' each other and physically embodying the two distinctive characters: monster and wizard.

Use a humorous element of surprise when playing Prospero, varying the rhythm and the pace with which you give Caliban the cramps. It is enjoyable, for example, to give the cramps immediately after you have said 'Better', allowing no time for Caliban to recover before he is writhing back on the floor. In this way you can repeat the game many times, allowing him to 'suffer' for longer extended periods and making the gap between cramps and 'Better' almost imperceptible. For some children the two commands become one and a gabbled, humorous 'Bettercramps' becomes a command all in itself.

Conversely you can reverse this pattern, allowing a short period of 'Caliban's suffering' and a long agonizing wait for the next cramps. This is equally enjoyable and allows the children to experience and explore the listening silence of anticipation together. Ideally the game has a combination of the two rhythms, with Prospero in complete control of the game, his power resting in nothing more than the rhythm with which he speaks. When you have played both roles with the child, come back to the circle to share.

Adding more words

The game can be played with longer phrases from each character.

Demonstration

Before playing memorize these lines

Prospero: I'll rack you with old cramps,

> Fill all thy bones with aches
> Make thee roar
Caliban: This island's mine
> by Sycorax my mother
> Which you took from me.
Prospero: Better

Two actors are in the circle as Caliban and Prospero exactly as before. They play the game adding all the words. It may be that Caliban has not finished before Prospero interrupts him with 'Better'. Prospero gives him three rounds of cramps and after some breathing space the players swap roles.

Playing with the children

Do not add the longer phrases until you have demonstrated, played and shared the game as it is set out in its initial simple form. If the full phrases are introduced too soon there is a danger that the game will become an exercise in managing words thereby lessening the impact of the sensory awareness. The heart of the game is the heightened anticipation shared between the players during the listening silences, punctuated by words not dominated by them. Ensure that the child experiences the game and then build in language accordingly.

Once you are happy to add the extra language use the rule of 'turning the volume of your voice down in relation to your emotions', the more intense the emotion the quieter your voice. This ensures you always have more to give and each turn of the game can be re-energized.

You can create another version for Prospero's lines by speaking the last word of each phrase, a useful acting tool for Shakespeare, saying this:

Cramps. Aches. Roar!

Quietly elongate the 'aw' sound within the roar to give another colour to Prospero's expressiveness.

Prospero may break the 'spell' with his command of 'Better' at any time and you can practise doing so before Caliban has come to the end of his phrase. This puts dramatic pressure on Caliban who must stop speaking, mid-phrase, immediately on the command. He must then remain soundless, until the next command of cramps.

When he resumes speaking, once more under the spell, he can pick up from where he broke off as if he has been holding the thoughts in his mind and now once the cramps return he continues to speak. It's a challenging version of the game, but really fun.

Once you have repeated the game several times, come back to the circle to share.

Four 'Shadow' games

These 'Shadow' games have the same structure as used for *A Midsummer Night's Dream*. They are classic games of 'he's behind you' adapted to challenge the children's difficulties, this time bringing the story of Caliban and Ariel to life. Whereas in *A Midsummer Night's Dream* the circle represented a forest, for *The Tempest* it becomes an island.

The 'Shadow' game

Prospero sends Ariel, a spirit who can fly, swim, dive into fire and ride on curled clouds to torment Caliban.

The game encourages physical co-ordination, increased spatial awareness and provides a transformative experience. No physical contact is ever made during the 'Shadow' games, the 'catching' is achieved with eye contact.

Demonstration

Two players stand together in the circle. They introduce themselves as Caliban and Ariel. Caliban assumes the stooped physical shape of a monster, curved and low, knees bent and with an angry facial expression. Ariel stands directly behind Caliban, an arm's distance away and assumes the same position, copying his hunched physicality; a perfect shadow. Keeping his body shape, Caliban slowly starts to move around the circle, and Ariel follows him, copying everything he is doing with as much precision as possible, whilst maintaining an arm's length distance behind him. Caliban is physically expressive with his stooped body, bringing the monster to life, scratching, stretching his arms, yawning and moving in different directions. He keeps his movements low and earth-bound, varying the speed in which he moves around the circle but, crucially, he never runs.

After a minute or two he senses that there is something behind him and begins to try to catch Ariel, at which point the game gains momentum as Ariel tries not to get caught. Caliban's 'anger' dissolves into 'fear' as he realizes Ariel is behind him and Ariel becomes increasingly 'daring'. When Caliban feels the time is up, he whips round to find Ariel and both players make a few seconds of eye contact at which point there is a natural intake of breath creating the game's Point of Ecstasy. The players then take a little breathing space before they swap parts and play again.

Playing with the children

All the guidance for playing the 'Shadow' games with the children in Part I is applicable here. It is essential reading if you are new to the games (see p. 24).

Use the stooped monster physicality of Caliban to challenge the children's physical stiffness and seeming inflexibility. It may be that a monster can stand up straight with unbent knees, creating a Frankenstein effect but Caliban is earth-bound, made of earth and water and you should encourage the children to embody his curved low shape. This is purposefully hard for the children, directly challenging their physical difficulties and pushing their boundaries through the enjoyable means of creating this character and playing the game.

I have noticed an unwillingness in children at both ends of the spectrum to bend their knees even though there's no obvious physical cause – their knee joints can and will move, it just takes a while for them to achieve it. Give the children encouragement, verbal and physical, directly helping them if appropriate. Connect yourself to the child's time frame rather than expecting them to meet yours. 'Take your time' is a phrase worth repeating more than almost any other – a beautiful, powerful phrase. Allow them to feel that you know they understand you and that they are doing their best to achieve the physical task.

For the 'Shadow' game both players will need to embody a stooped, curved physical life, bending their knees and keeping them bent throughout the game as they move around the circle. Encourage them to copy you, the combination of demonstration and encouragement is essential; do not under any circumstance find yourself standing upright whilst saying 'Bend your knees', and expecting the child to obey. Use your instructive playfulness to allow the child to learn through copying you, not through following orders.

If they can only maintain the physicality for brief periods of time, allow the game to be played for short turns, taking breaks and swapping roles regularly. The 'Shadow' game should always be fun, the excitement of hiding behind another person whilst trying not to get caught, culminating with a moment of eye contact is paramount every time.

When you have repeated the game several times, come back to the circle to share.

The 'Shadow' game, with invisible Ariel

In this next version Ariel has become invisible, freezing like a statue when Caliban turns round to find her. Caliban turns round three times but only catches her out with the third.

Demonstration

Begin as before with two actors in the circle, Ariel an arm's distance behind Caliban, both assuming the stooped monster shape. Ariel shadows Caliban around the circle maintaining the same distance behind him and copying all his movements. Only this time Ariel is invisible. The first time Caliban turns round, Ariel freezes like a statue in whatever position she is in. Caliban stares into Ariel's eyes for a few seconds, and Ariel doesn't move a muscle. Caliban becomes confused and decides to carry on moving around the island. As soon as he turns away to continue around the circle, Ariel unfreezes and returns to following him as his shadow. No moment is ever to be rushed.

Caliban then turns round to catch Ariel a second time and they repeat the same 'freezing' action. Increasingly confused, Caliban turns away again and on his third and final attempt, he whips round very fast and catches her before Ariel has the chance to freeze. They both make true eye contact providing the POE. After a breathing space the partners swap roles and play again.

Playing with the children

All the same tips for playing the 'Shadow' game are applicable here. The moment of looking into Ariel's 'invisible eyes' should be explored fully, especially with those who have the cognitive ability to understand the concept of invisibility. Encourage Ariel to mimic the monster as best she can so that when she freezes it is as though Caliban is looking at a reflection of himself. Although she is invisible!

When you have repeated the game a few times, return to the circle to share.

The 'Shadow' game with playful Ariel

In this version Ariel wildly exaggerates all Caliban's movements, whilst still shadowing him and avoiding being caught.

Demonstration

Two actors stand in the circle and begin as before with Ariel an arm's length behind Caliban ready to shadow him, both players assuming the stooped Monster position. The rhythm of the game remains the same – Caliban moves around the circle being shadowed by Ariel and he tries to 'catch' Ariel three times. Ariel freezes for the first two and is caught at the third creating the POE. In this version it is the shadowing itself which is different, Ariel now exaggerates the movements of the monster Caliban, picking up on a tiny gesture or movement or sensation and creating a bigger version of it. A small scratch from Caliban becomes a big scraping movement from Ariel. A little shrug from Caliban becomes an exaggerated one from Ariel. A roll on the floor from Caliban becomes a double roll from Ariel. This released exaggeration creates a heightened moment of humour each time Ariel has to freeze.

Playing with the children

Refer back to the notes from Part I (p. 24) especially if you have not played the 'Shadow' games before. Encourage the children to think of Ariel as a giant threatening shadow looming higher and bigger behind Caliban with every move. Maintain a playful and humorous undercurrent to the game, ensuring that the children find moments of listening silence and stillness within each turn. When you have repeated the game a few times, return to the circle to share.

The 'Shadow' game with flying Ariel

In this version Ariel flies, swims, dives into fire and rides on curled clouds. Her transformative life force is released and although ostensibly she is still Caliban's shadow, her physicality reveals her wild-spirited essence.

Demonstration

Two actors stand in the circle and begin as before with Ariel an arm's length behind Caliban ready to shadow him. The rhythm of the game remains the same, Caliban walks around the circle being shadowed by Ariel and he tries to 'catch' Ariel three times. Ariel freezes for the first two and is caught at the third creating the POE. It's important that Ariel still follows Caliban around the circle and remains behind him at all times trying not to be seen. However, instead of any attempt to copy or exaggerate Caliban's movements, Ariel now flies, swims, dives into fires and rides clouds like a silent wild spirit, leaping, swooping, surfing the air to her heart's content, keeping Caliban in her vision at all times, so that she can freeze as soon as Caliban turns around. As always, the partners should take a breathing space before swapping roles and playing again. The pure abandon and joy with which these movements are demonstrated is vital if the children are to emulate it.

Playing with the children

If explored carefully the four instructional verbs – fly, swim, dive and ride – create a dance-like experience for the children. Explore the actions in whatever way you choose: concentrating on just one, a swimming Ariel is great fun, a combination, flying and diving can be very releasing, or all four. Encourage a sense of physical freedom within the child playing Ariel, which she can express throughout her whole body. The dramatic comedy of the game is provided every time she has to freeze and Caliban catches her in impossible physical positions in which she must try as hard as she can to remain motionless.

However if the child topples over unbalanced when playing, then all the better; gently falling over within the safe environment of a game is no bad thing, in fact later on in the book there is a game wholly dedicated to falling over. When you have practised a few times, return to the circle to share your flying Ariel with the group.

Sounds and shadows

Under Prospero's command Ariel torments Caliban by changing from a biting ape to a prickled hedgehog to a hissing adder.

This version of the 'Shadow' game incorporates these three creatures, the ape, the hedgehog and the adder providing an opportunity for the children to challenge their vocal difficulties using sound.

Demonstration

Before playing memorize these sounds

Ariel
Chattering ape: OO-OO-A-A-A-A-A-A-A *(low and chattering, teeth bared)*
Hedgehog: Mi-mi-mi-mi-mi *(high pitched as possible)*
Adder: Sss-sss-sss-sss-sss- *(hissing, rhythmic and increasingly fast)*
Caliban: I'll fall flat

Two actors stand in the circle, Ariel standing an arm's length behind Caliban, who has assumed the stooping monster shape ready to play. As Caliban begins to move, Ariel shadows him but this time she transforms herself into the shape of the first creature – the ape. She beats her fists on her chest, strong and powerful and when she chooses, she makes the sound of the ape, low and chattering, teeth bared. When Caliban hears the sound he turns round and Ariel freezes in whatever 'ape-like' position she has been found in.

After a few seconds of looking at (and through) Ariel, Caliban returns to moving around the circle and Ariel returns to shadowing him, this time assuming the shape of the hedgehog. Remaining on her feet, her entire body becomes spiky and jagged as if this hedgehog is threatening to stab Caliban with her prickles. The repetitive 'mi-mi-mi' sound should be almost imperceptible, like a bat. When Ariel makes the sound, Caliban turns round and Ariel freezes in her 'hedgehog' shape. After looking in her eyes, Caliban turns away and continues fearfully around the circle.

Now Ariel assumes the shape of the adder, palms together, remaining on her feet and becoming tall, thin and wispy, with smooth silky movement. Ariel hisses in Caliban's ear and Caliban turns around to catch her. Fearful for his life he exclaims:

> I'll fall flat

and falls to the floor, lying flat as he can, face down and hiding. This line and action provide the POE for the game.

After some breathing space, the players swap roles and play again.

Playing with the children

Practise the sounds with the children and ensure that they achieve as much variety as possible within the demands of three different creatures. Encourage them to stretch their vocal range, exploring the difference in register between the low chatter of the monkey and impossibly high squeal of the hedgehog, culminating in the quiet hissing ssss of the adder. Ensure that the children embody the physical life of the creature with such vigour that they create a personal need to express themselves with sound and when the sound comes it is inextricably linked to the movements the child is embodying. Encouraging the children to connect their physical life with the impulse to make sound is essential and fundamental for all the games in the book.

Most of the children's voices 'stay on the same note', therefore their vocal chords have never been thoroughly exercised, but it is not enough to merely offer abstract training for their voices. Some of these children remain non-verbal for many years and when they do finally speak it is often with an unfamiliar quality as if what they are saying doesn't belong to them. What the children need is to connect the sound of their own voices to their thoughts and feelings and thereby experience the power of vocal ownership. Encouraging them to play this deceptively simple game, allowing their voices to emerge as a result of their direct physical experience, marks a playful beginning to a serious endeavour.

Beware. I played this game with a group of children in New York City, amongst whom was a young girl, practically non-verbal, who loved the games and tried them all with enthusiasm. She enjoyed this game very much and on her second day of playing she took the role of Caliban. At the end of her turn, she raised her arms high above her head exclaiming 'I'll fall flat' and proceeded to launch her body as flat as an ironing board toward the ground, heading for a catastrophic collision as her forehead hurtled toward the solid floor. Every one of us present in the room launched ourselves toward her and she landed, flat as a pancake upon a cushion of our bodies. That morning I learnt that the children will sometimes take Shakespeare's words literally and that a group of people can move very quickly when they need to.

When the children have repeated this game a few times, come back to the circle to share.

Toads, beetles, bats

> All the charms
> Of Sycorax, toads, beetles, bats, light on you
> *(The Tempest*, I, ii, 406–7)

Caliban dreams of taking revenge on Prospero, and in the name of his mother, the witch Sycorax, he curses his master.

This is a version of the 'Shadow' game, which provides Caliban with the chance to express his desires having been tormented by Prospero and Ariel in every game so far. It works well as a group activity, with a sole Prospero being shadowed by a group of Calibans. The game targets the children's spatial awareness and provides an excellent transformative experience.

Demonstration

Before playing memorize these lines

Caliban: Toads, beetles, bats
Prospero: Abominable monster
             Caliban

Two actors stand in the circle. One is Prospero, tall and commanding as the wizard. Behind him, an arm's distance away is Caliban, squatting down on his haunches, hands on the floor in front of him, in the shape of a toad. Prospero begins to move around the circle, slowly and with long strides. Caliban shadows him, hopping like a toad and after a few seconds he quietly says with a menacing voice:

Toads

Prospero hears but keeps moving around the circle without turning round. Immediately after this Caliban, still shadowing Prospero, jumps up to his feet, knees bent, transforming into the shape of a beetle. His arms and hands tight to his body, his fingers moving like claws. With this movement he says:

Beetles

Again Prospero hears but keeps moving around the circle and finally Caliban jumps as high into the air as he can, arms above his head exclaiming:

Bats

At this Prospero whips round to find Caliban, but Caliban has made himself as small as possible, curled up in a ball at Prospero's feet. Prospero looks everywhere but down, speaking very slowly and with menace:

Abominable monster

This marks the end of one round, the whole thing should take no more than ten seconds. When Prospero turns back to continue round the circle, Caliban resumes his toad-like shape and the game begins again. The players play three times. Each bat's leap provides a POE.

At the third round Prospero catches Caliban's eyes and slowly says:

Caliban

After some breathing space the players swap roles and play again.

Playing with the children

The speed of Caliban's transformative change between the three creatures makes the game enjoyable, especially if the distinctive differences are as fully realized as possible. Encourage the child to experience the expressive physical progression from low toad to mid-height beetle and culminating with the leaping bat. Each 'bat leap' provides a release of energy for a split second as if Caliban is escaping his imprisonment. Ensure that the experience of playing the two characters is significantly different, thereby exploring the sense of danger that Caliban creates by teasing Prospero.

When you have repeated the game a few times come back to the circle to share.

Demonstration/playing with the group

Once you have played in pairs you can explore the game as a whole group. Everyone is on their feet inside the circle, one actor is Prospero with an upright commanding stance and the rest of the group play Caliban, assuming the shape of the toad to begin. If a child needs assistance, then an actor can guide her by staying close and giving encouragement, holding hands or physically assisting if needed. Prospero begins to move around the whole room, followed by the Calibans. In unison the Calibans make their toads, beetles, bats, exactly as before, culminating with the whole group leaping up for the bat leap and then curling up to hide when Prospero turns round, saying 'Caliban' and finishing the game. Ensure that all the children have a turn as Prospero, either alone or assisted by an actor if necessary.

With each round of toads, beetles, bats Caliban's sense of danger increases in intensity, as does Prospero's irritation and arrogance. These dynamics of character should be explored fully by the whole group to ensure that the game does not descend into a mere exercise of moving around the room en masse. Encourage everybody to 'breathe together' as a group; it is the collective shared silences in between the words which create intimacy when working in unison, out of which everyone instinctively knows when to speak.

Use the technique of turning your volume down with increasing emotions and ensure that the children are listening to each other's voices, not just their own. This game is very exciting if the whole group whisper in unison, but very dull if the whole group are shouting. Explore the quiet explosive 't' and 'b' sounds at the beginning of Caliban's words in order to bring his increasing sense of danger to life.

Teaching Caliban to speak

> I pitied thee
> Took pains to make thee speak, taught thee each hour
> One thing or other. When thou didst not, savage,
> Know thine own meaning, but wouldst gabble like
> A thing most brutish
>
> (*The Tempest*, I, ii, 424–9)

When Miranda arrives on the island she teaches the savage Caliban to speak, stroking him, making much of him and naming for him the sun and the moon.

This game is an imagined version of their encounter, exploring their tutor/pupil relationship, which also has connotations of a parent/child bond and further suggestion of a deep rapport between friends. The moment that Caliban learns his name offers a beautiful POE shared by both players. At its best, this game provides a transformative acting opportunity for the actors and children to engage with each other, physically, vocally and emotionally. The inherent element of improvisation – resulting in the game never being the same twice – can provide a liberating experience for the child, but at the same time requires a high level of acting ability and initiative from both players.

Demonstration

Before playing memorize these words

Miranda: My name is Miranda
             Your name is Caliban

Two actors are in the circle, one is Caliban who assumes the shape of a savage monster, the other is Miranda, watching him. Both are sitting on the floor. Caliban is gabbling, making noise with no language. He is moving around the circle on all fours, making a never-ending clamorous babble. Miranda approaches Caliban in an attempt to teach him to speak. She attracts his attention with kindness and, pointing to herself she slowly says:

My name is Mi … ran … da

Caliban continues to babble through her talking, but he also begins to listen. Miranda continues, pointing to him:

> Your name is Ca … li … ban, Caliban

Caliban's babbling decreases, he understands that he is meant to speak and he tries to make the first sound. Miranda is encouraging him, repeating the sound, but when he tries, all he can make is his babbling.

Miranda tries again, pointing to him:

> Your name is Ca … li … ban, Caliban

And once more Caliban tries to say his name but makes only a babbling sound.

This continues for five or six goes, until Caliban manages to say:

> Ca

Miranda is delighted, she praises Caliban and now continues to teach him his name, splitting it into its three parts:

> Ca … li … ban.

It takes Caliban a few more goes to move from babbling to speaking his name and with each successful attempt, Miranda is increasingly happy and gives him more praise. After about two minutes (three at the most) Caliban can speak his name and they both rejoice. Both players take a breathing space, swap roles and play again.

Before you split into pairs, one actor stays in the circle as Caliban, babbling as a savage. Invite children one by one to come into the circle as Miranda to teach him to speak. Each time he has learnt his name, they share their delight and the child leaves the circle. Caliban then resumes his babbling as if he has immediately forgotten his name again, and you call the next child into the circle to teach him. Continue until all the children have played. They can come accompanied by an actor if needed.

Playing with the children

Of all the games in the book this is the most complex, demanding an imaginative leap and independence of mind from both players. Do not attempt the game if you feel the child cannot grasp the fundamental concepts, you will only be frustrated. If the child is on the cusp of comprehending the game, enlist another adult or child to play with you so that you can play as a duo, using prompting for support.

PLAYING MIRANDA

The child playing Miranda will experience the emotional roller-coaster between success and failure as well as a feeling of power and knowledge. Encourage them to play this role first, whilst you play Caliban and give them something savage and humorous to work against. Develop your own physical and vocal version of the babbling Caliban, everyone's will be unique – mine has a strong element of a Jack Russell dog in it – and make the child work hard to get you to speak.

If the child needs help with the game you can pair up to play Miranda together, which has the surreal effect of you teaching the child to teach Caliban to speak. For some children this is a very enjoyable and useful experience and provides their only means of accessing the game.

PLAYING CALIBAN

Ensure that the child understand the demands of playing Caliban; they must take initiative in the role, autonomously choosing when to progress from babbling to speaking whilst staying in character. If the child needs your support whilst you are playing Miranda ensure that you use instructive playfulness, prompting them to speak the next sound whilst you as Miranda teach it, swapping seamlessly between being the facilitator and playing Miranda. Again, this can be a surreal experience, but it develops from care and attention to the child's needs; at the heart of the work you are pinpointing what the child can't do, and doing it with them until they can. Alternatively you can pair up with the child creating a 'two-headed Caliban' and prompting the child to move through the language changes together. In both cases your instructive playfulness is the key to success.

It may be useful to lay down a limit of two minutes duration for a child to play the babbling monster – use a clock or watch if you want to – clearly telling them that the game will be over by then, whether or not Caliban has learnt his name. A few children enjoy the babbling so much that they wilfully refuse to stop, and if after a few attempts they can't move on from the babbling, abandon the game. The two-minute clock strategy works wonders for any game if the child has issues with time.

When you have played both roles, come back to the circle to share.

Adding more words

Demonstration/playing with children

Before playing memorize these words

Miranda: Sun
           Moon

Demonstrate, play and share the game exactly as before with the addition of 'sun' and 'moon'. Immediately after Caliban has learnt his name, Miranda points to the sky and teaches him the word 'sun'. She physicalizes heat and the scale of the sun with her arms, body and voice, highlighting the hissing sound of the word, doing everything she can to make Caliban understand. After a minute of wavering between babble and language he says the word 'Sun' with a long emphasis on the hissing sound of the 's' and finishing with a triumphant 'n'. Miranda and Caliban share a moment of celebration, repeating the word 'sun' together and pointing to it in the sky.

She then does the same for 'moon', emphasizing the long 'oo' sound, like a howling wolf. Again it takes Caliban about one minute to learn 'moon', progressing from babbling through to speaking and then celebrating his success with Miranda. They can now speak their names and point to the sun and moon, which offers more scope for improvisation between the two players.

Hello, too close, goodbye

> thou didst seek to violate
> The honour of my child
>
> ...
>
> O ho! O ho! Would't had been done!
> Thou didst prevent me. I had peopled else
> This isle with Calibans
>
> (*The Tempest*, I, ii, 417–21)

Having been given the gift of language by Miranda, Caliban wants her for himself, desiring to people the island with Calibans. Prospero makes Caliban his slave to protect his daughter.

I choose not to tackle this narrative directly, but this game provides a palatable means for the children to explore their physical boundaries. Difficulties with spatial awareness and interpreting physical boundaries can cause problems for the children when they are young, and these problems are often exacerbated during the teenage years. This game directly tackles these issues.

Demonstration

Before playing memorize these lines

Caliban: Hello Ho Ho
Miranda: Too close No No
            Goodbye Go Go

Two actors are in the circle, one is Caliban who assumes his stooped monster shape and a hopeful facial expression. The other is Miranda, upright and strong with a disgusted facial expression. They stand one pace away from each other and they make eye contact.

Caliban takes one step in toward Miranda, stretching his face up toward hers and standing 'too close for comfort'. His feet, face and body are a centimetre away from hers, as close as he can be without touching. Miranda's feet are pinned to the floor and she must endure his close uncomfortable presence. He says with his monstrous voice:

Hello Ho Ho

They stand in this uncomfortable position for a few seconds and Miranda says:

> Too close No No

She then takes one step sideways or backwards away from Caliban saying:

> Goodbye Go Go

This marks the end of the sequence.

Caliban begins again, taking one step toward Miranda so that he stands opposite her again. Once more he stands too close for comfort saying:

> Hello Ho Ho

and the sequence begins again as above. They repeat the sequence three more times. With each repetition Caliban becomes more hopeful whilst Miranda becomes increasingly disgusted. Finally Miranda turns her back on Caliban with her last sidestep and Caliban defeated and sad says:

> Goodbye

He emphasizes the 'bye' and this sad ending provides a POE to the game.

The actors in the Ohio research project created an alternative 'happy' ending:

On the last sequence Caliban finally gets the idea and stands an appropriate distance from Miranda. She loses her disgusted face and she does not say 'Too close', but instead she smiles and says:

> Hello

Caliban and Miranda smile together and say in unison:

> Hello!

This provides the game with the POE.

Playing with the children

The regulated pattern of the game with its single steps backwards and sideways provides the children with a formula they can hold onto whilst exploring the game's essential challenge – tackling physical boundaries. If the children find it very difficult to move backwards, stick to the sideways move. The aim of the game is to explore the moment of close discomfort between you and the child. Ensure when you are playing Caliban that you get as close to the child as you possibly can without touching. The moment will feel invasive, but if you exaggerate Caliban's hopefulness you will also find the humour that underpins the game. A hopeful monster may well be a grossly disgusting monster and you can invent snorting, scratching and even burping to bring this grotesque character to life, a centimetre away from the child's face. Ideally you will make them laugh at the same time as making them want to move.

When you are playing Miranda, do not speak her words until the child is as close to you as possible. Remain silent, gesturing with your hands that they, as Caliban, need to come closer, and only stopping them when they are a centimetre away. If they keep stopping in their comfort zone and saying 'Hello Ho Ho', that is fine but ensure that you can only say 'Too close' when they are in fact too close. It may be that this becomes a game in itself.

If you want to use the game to teach the children about boundaries – you may have a child who could benefit from this direct approach – you should explore the second 'happy' ending, in which Caliban purposefully takes a comfortable distance from Miranda and they both say a smiling 'Hello' together. However, this 'happy ending' does not fit the play's narrative and you should make a distinction between this version and the first wherein Caliban is rejected. Both versions are valid.

When you have repeated the game a few times come back to the circle to share.

Gibberish

> You taught me language and my profit on 't
> Is I know how to curse
>
> (*The Tempest*, I, ii, 437–8)

Caliban's rage against Prospero continues throughout the play. This game provides an excellent means for them to express their anger toward each other. The game is essentially an exchange of insults between two players where the language used is gibberish. It focuses on basic patterns of inflection, teaching the children that inflection gives communicative meaning to language. The game provides an opportunity to explore listening and responding by practising how and when to inflect words. The humour of the game is to be found in the contrast between the seriousness with which the players take the insults and the silliness of the sounds they make.

Demonstration

Two players are in the circle face to face, a few paces from each other. When they speak, they will use only gibberish, no comprehensible words are allowed. One player is Prospero and the other is Caliban. Prospero begins by calling Caliban an insulting 'gibberish' name making it obvious from his vocal inflection and his body language that he is giving him an insult. His gibberish is short and repeatable. Caliban hears the gibberish word and immediately repeats it, as if outraged by the insult and making it obvious from his inflection that he is appalled by what he hears. He repeats it several times as if he can't believe his ears.

Caliban now calls Prospero an insulting gibberish name, making it obvious from his inflection that he has given him an insult. The gibberish is short and repeatable. Prospero hears the gibberish word and immediately repeats it as if doubly outraged by the insult and making it obvious from his inflection that he is appalled by what he hears. He repeats it several times as if he can't believe his ears.

Both players now take turns to give and receive gibberish insults to each other, ensuring that each time they receive an insult they immediately repeat it out loud – as if in outrage – creating a POE on each repetition. The players physically characterize the outrage with their body language to support their vocal expressiveness. As the game continues they increase the length, complexity and intensity of the insults with each one that is invented.

The leader brings the game to a close after a few minutes play.

Playing with the children

When we are spoken to we immediately process what we hear and construct an answer, which we then speak. This process is usually in silence. Receiving the gibberish and repeating it several times is a vocal externalization of that process and is the key moment of the game. Encourage the children to explore this moment as slowly as they like, allowing the activity to bring them into the present, compelling them in a humorous and enjoyable way to communicate with their partner.

If the child understands the game and can make up their own words ensure that you can give them increasingly interesting and difficult things to repeat. Invent patterns of sound and rhythm that challenge their language skills. Be ready for anything they throw at you and repeat it with a deadly seriousness – it is wonderful if the child is finding it funny, but guard against laughing yourself whilst you are playing, however hilarious it may be. Save your laughter for talking about the experience with the child after you have played.

If the child is unable to make up insults either prompt them yourself or elicit another adult to whisper ideas into their ear. Use simple alliterative phrases to begin with, for example 'Bu-bu-dee-bah' is a perfect example of a gibberish insult, which can be repeated and inflected in an infinite variety of ways. You can also experiment with different vocal techniques, rolling 'R's, clicking your tongue and making a 'Brrrr' with your lips. Give the children clear instruction that the rules of the game don't allow them to use any real words.

When you have repeated the game a few times come back to the circle to share.

Using Shakespeare's words

You can play the exact same game using Shakespeare's insults to bring Caliban and Prospero to life.

Demonstration

Before playing memorize these insults

Prospero:	Freckled whelp!
	Hag seed!
	Abhorred slave!
	Savage!
Caliban:	Tyrant!
	Meddling monkey!

Two players are in the circle face to face, a few paces from each other. One player is Prospero and the other is Caliban. Play the game exactly as before but this time use the words above to replace the gibberish.

Playing with the children

Ensure that the children stick to Shakespeare's insults and that you use this version to further develop their exploration of inflection. When you have repeated the game and the child has played both roles come back to the circle to share.

Chapter 8

Ariel

I come
To answer thy best pleasure, be't to fly
To swim, to dive into the fire, to ride
On the curled clouds

(The Tempest, I, ii, 224–7)*

An exploration of Ariel is an exploration of Shakespeare's magic. She is a spirit of fire and air, freed from her pine tree prison by her master, and fixed on the idea of liberty. Each of these games represents a task she must perform at Prospero's bidding, demanding various acts of transformation, physical, vocal and emotional.

The games

- I go, I go
- Throwing the flame
- Ferdinand
- Ariel's Trance
- How now? Moody?

The characters

- Ariel
- Prospero
- Ferdinand
- Miranda

The targets

- Physical engagement
- Spatial awareness
- Facial expressiveness
- Exploration of feeling

I go, I go.

Ariel willingly performs Prospero's bidding saying 'I go, I go' in answer to his commands and as an expression of her longing for liberty. This game is in fact an extended version of the Heartbeat Circle using the pulsing rhythm to express Ariel's desire for freedom.

Play immediately after the 'Hello heartbeats' and before 'Throwing the face'. When paired with the next game – 'Throwing the flame' – you can introduce the children to the storm, the tempest of the play.

Demonstration/playing with the children

Before playing memorize these words

    I go

Immediately after the Heartbeat Circle, all the actors become Ariel, kneeling up on the floor, assuming an alert expression. Their hands are on their hearts, beating the 'Heartbeat' rhythm on their chests – which they maintain collectively for the whole game. With the rhythm established, one by one around the circle each actor says:

    I go

making a tiny bounce upwards as if becoming ready to jump. With each actor the bounce increases a little in height and excitement until finally they are leaping into the air, quietly exclaiming 'I go', and coming straight back down to their place in the circle. When they leap, the hand that is beating the heartbeat releases high up in the air on the word 'go'. Finish the demonstration after a few rounds of high leaping from all the actors.

Now invite the children to join in as Ariel. Everyone around the circle sits up on their knees, hands on hearts, ready to play.

Begin the game again exactly as before, establish the rhythm of the heartbeat and then one by one around the circle – this time allowing the children to take their turn as Ariel – everyone says 'I go', accompanied by a small bouncing movement, increasing with each round and culminating in the whole group leaping one at a time with the quiet exclamation of 'I go'. Each leap provides a POE.

If the children are unable to take their turn by themselves, pair up with them and take a turn together. Increase the speed of the rhythm, keeping it even and steady to create an increasingly exciting circle, everybody leaping higher each time.

Finish when you have taken the final leap, and allow everyone to sit back down. After some breathing space follow immediately with 'Throwing the flame' in order to create the storm of the play.

Throwing the flame

> I board'd the King's ship, now on the beak,
> Now in the waist, the deck, in every cabin
> I flam'd amazement. Sometime I'd divide
> And burn in many places – on the topmast,
> The yards and bowsprit would I flame distinctly
> Then meet and join.
>
> (*The Tempest*, I, ii, 232–7)

At Prospero's demand, Ariel creates a tempest out at sea, destroying a ship and shipwrecking its passengers.

The game uses the same technique as 'Throwing the face' but this time encompasses the whole body.

Demonstration/playing with the children

Immediately after playing 'I go, I go', everyone stands up around the circle. One actor becomes Ariel. Staying on the spot, she moves her body as if it is a flame of fire, rapidly blowing out tiny breaths of air and moving her limbs in all directions with speed and precision. It should not be a mess, but rather the human embodiment of a single blazing flame of fire.

Ariel continues to make the flame and an actor on the opposite side of the room becomes the 'catcher'. Once Ariel and the catcher are ready, give the instruction of '1, 2, 3 Throw the flame' at which

Ariel throws her flame with her whole body, jumping a little off the ground with the effort, and the catcher 'catches' it, immediately alive and febrile, entirely animated by the life of the flame.

Use the same instruction of '1, 2, 3 Throw the flame' to play the game with the whole group around the circle, always ensuring that thrower and catcher are ready and making eye contact before they play. Mix the game up so that the flame is thrown to pairs and small groups, and finally to the group as a whole, creating an entire circle of flaming Ariels before finishing back with the original actor. It is fun to ask the group to blow her flame out! If children are unable to play by themselves when the flame is thrown, pair up with them and take a turn together.

Ferdinand

> The King's son Ferdinand
> With hair up-staring (then like reeds, not hair)
> Was the first man that leapt, cried 'Hell is empty
> And all the devils are here'.
> ...
> The King's son have I landed by himself
> Whom I left cooling of the air with sighs
> In an odd angle of the isle, and sitting
> His arms in this sad knot.
>
> (*The Tempest*, I, ii, 250–3, 262–5)

The King's son Ferdinand is on board the flaming ship and leaps into the sea to save himself. This introduction to his character should be played immediately after 'Throwing the flame'.

The game marks a significant development from previous 'Throwing' games in which the technique of copying is used, and both thrower and catcher play the same character. In this game the thrower is Ariel and the catcher is Ferdinand.

Demonstration

With everyone still standing up around the circle after 'Throwing the flame', one actor assumes the shape of Ariel as the flame of fire. The second actor plays Ferdinand, he is on the opposite side of the circle, staring at Ariel. On the instruction of '1, 2, 3 Throw the flame' Ariel throws the flame to Ferdinand who immediately becomes animated by fire and pulls his hair up as far as he can (then like reeds, not hair), leaps to his tiptoes and leaning to one side as if looking overboard with a terrified face he exclaims:

> Hell is empty and all the devils are here

As he says 'here', he elongates the vowel sound, leaps up and 'swims' with his arms in the air. Landing back down on the ground, he sits curled up as tightly as possible, assuming a sad face gazing upwards toward the sky, his arms in a 'sad knot'. His leap on the word 'here' provides the POE.

They swap roles and play again. Play this game as a group activity a few times in order to learn the words. It is then important to split into pairs and small groups to explore the idea of catching a face, body and voice without the prop of copying.

Playing with the children

If the child struggles with the concept of playing a part, and only responds to copying your actions, enlist another adult or child to play with you and team up as a duo, giving the child hands-on physical help if necessary. If there is no help on hand, explore each role separately, encouraging the child to experience the physical transformation from being themselves to embodying either Ariel or Ferdinand and then being themselves again using instructions.

This is a version of 'Playing a part' from the games of *A Midsummer Night's Dream* and if the child likes it and understands the concept you can use it as an alternative way of introducing any character.

For example.

Ariel

Standing in a plain and simple way the child says:

> My name is Jack and I'm playing Ariel

He assumes Ariel's animated body of flame.
He then speaks with Ariels voice:

> I'm Ariel and I'm throwing my flame of fire

He throws the flame.

He returns to standing in a plain and simple way saying:

> And now I'm Jack again.

Ferdinand

Standing in a plain and simple way the child says:

> My name is Lucy and I'm playing Ferdinand

She assumes Ferdinand's animated body, hair upstanding like reeds, not hair.

Then speaks with Ferdinand's voice:

> I'm Ferdinand and I'm leaping from the ship

She leaps up and lands on the floor, her arms in the sad knot.

After a few seconds she stands again, in a plain and simple way, saying:

> And now I'm Lucy again

It may be enough to embody just one role for one session and tackle the other at a later date. Take your time with children who struggle with cognition, and adapt each game to suit their needs; every time the child makes a physical transformation, no matter how much support they have received from you in order to make it, is another step toward their communicative progress.

If the children comprehend the game, ensure they understand that the two characters are fundamentally different, one is magical and the other is not. Encourage them to explore the distinction between Ferdinand, a terrified human who ends the game curled up in a sad knot on the floor, and Ariel, a spirit of fire and air able to split herself into a thousand flames.

The notion of magic may cause problems for some of the more literal-minded children. One boy from the Ohio research project encapsulated this for me whilst playing this game. He was happy to take part and was beautifully expressive in his interpretation of both characters but he was perturbed at the very idea of magic, claiming that 'it's not logical'. To which I replied, as I quote at the beginning of this section 'You're right, it's not logical ... it's magic'. He had no answer to this, but for a boy who finds a scientific reasoning to everything my answer seemed to give him much food for thought.

It's worth remembering why this may be important. Perhaps the denial of magic is the denial of imagination, which is in itself the denial of our dream world, or at the very least a fear of expressing it. I would never tackle these fears and beliefs with direct questions but in undertaking these games it's interesting how questions of logic and magic emerge naturally for the children, as if the games empower them to initiate questions and grapple with these thoughts themselves. This lies at the heart of the work, the fundamental aim of which is to use Shakespeare as a means of waking the children up to their own lives. The plays ask more questions than they give answers and, at best, the work empowers the children to do the same, taking enquiring steps into unknown personal territory, which they would otherwise not have the opportunity to do.

When you have practised and repeated this game several times and are ready to share, come back to the circle.

Ariel's trance

> Full fathom five thy father lies
> Of his bones are coral made
> Those are pearls that were his eyes
> Nothing of him that doth fade
> But doth suffer a sea change
> Into something rich and strange
> Sea nymphs hourly ring his knell
> Ding dong
> Hark now I hear them: Ding dong bell
> (*The Tempest*, I, ii, 474–82)

Ferdinand is shipwrecked, believing his loved ones to be drowned, and at Prospero's command Ariel uses her magic to lead him to Miranda. Ariel's song purposefully awakens Ferdinand's grief and passions, stirring a depth of emotion within him just before he sets eyes on Miranda. The song has three key phrases – the bark of watch dogs, the crowing cock and the bells of sea-nymphs, evoking the sounds of awakening, dawn and death.

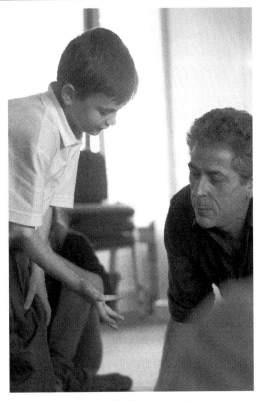

Photo 13 The Trance game (photo © Nick Spratling)

This game is a version of 'Puck's trance' from Part I (p. 42), a classic drama game adapted to combat the difficulties of autism; it directly challenges the children's spatial awareness and simultaneously offers further opportunity for focusing the eye. The use of sound in this version adds an emotional, mystical tone to the game, with Ferdinand wondering if the sounds come from the air or the earth. His text, spoken whilst being 'hypnotized' develops the game further and provides an additional challenge for the children.

Demonstration

Before playing memorize these lines

Ariel: Bow-wow
            Cock a diddle dow

Ding dong, ding dong bell
Ferdinand: Where should this music be? I'th'air? Or th'earth?
It sounds no more, tis gone
No, it begins again

Two actors will play, one is Ferdinand and the other Ariel. Ferdinand begins the game sitting in the circle, his arms in his 'sad knot'. Ariel stands in front of him, just an arm's length from him. She places the palm of her hand in front of Ferdinand's face. The distance should be comfortable for both players, ideally one hand span away; any closer is intimidating and any further away lessens the impact of the game. Ferdinand looks up into the palm of Ariel's hand as if hypnotized. Both players concentrate on keeping an equal distance between eyes and hand for the duration of the game; it is as if Ferdinand's eyes are transfixed by a magnetic force in the palm of Ariel's hand.

Ariel slowly begins to move her hand in any direction she chooses, maintaining her palm in the same position to Ferdinand's face at all times. As she moves, Ferdinand follows the palm of her hand with his eyes, smoothly re-positioning his head and body as much as he needs in order to maintain eye contact with the hand, Ariel raising her hand high so that Ferdinand must rise up out of his 'sad knot' sitting position.

Ariel's movements slowly grow to encompass her whole body until she begins to move slowly around the circle. Ferdinand follows her as if pulled by the invisible magnetic force, staring at all times into the palm of Ariel's hand. When she walks backwards, Ferdinand is seemingly pulled forward and if she moves forward, Ferdinand is pushed hypnotically backwards. The players slowly continue this magic 'push and pull' while Ariel begins to make her sounds. She uses her voice quietly and slowly, invoking the resonances of dawn, summoning the reverberations of an early morning landscape as though her vocal sound were an echo.

Bow-wow
Cock a diddle dow
Ding dong, ding dong bell

The physical game is smooth and continuous, a never-ending flow between the two players. In opposition to this Ariel varies the sounds, stopping and starting them as she pleases. When the sounds stop Ferdinand speaks:

> Where should this music be? I'th'air? Or th'earth?
> It sounds no more, tis gone

And when Ariel begins her sound again he says:

> No, it begins again

They continue playing in this way for a few minutes, and when Ariel has had enough she gently makes one handclap, which breaks the 'spell'. At the handclap both players take a breath together and share a moment of eye contact, creating a POE. They immediately swap roles. An alternative to the handclap is for Ariel to gently blow air onto Ferdinand's forehead as if to wake him from the trance. The demonstration is over when both players have played both parts.

Playing with the children

Play with the children according to their needs and understanding; the guidance and help for 'Puck's trance' in Part I (p. 43) is essential reading if you have not played the game before. Begin by playing without text or sound, ensuring that the child is able to comprehend the game and establishing for yourselves what level of help they need from you in order to play. Continue in this way until you feel comfortable adding sound.

Use your own vocal range and sensitivity to demonstrate and play with the children – your voice is the model for them to copy. Encourage them to fully explore their own quality of voice and feeling to create Ariel's 'echoes of dawn'. Make a distinction in vocal range and register between a low 'Bow wow', a high crowing 'Cock a diddle dow' and the faraway 'Ding dong bell', which should have a 'singsong' quality, the bells of sea-nymphs.

I have seen this game played where the soulfulness of voice has not been present and the game becomes a mere exercise of repeating noises, reducing the expressive experience of playing to zero. Ensure that Ferdinand's sadness is present before the game begins, the 'sad knot' of his body evoking his belief that he is alone in the world. This is met by Ariel's evocative soulfulness, which she uses in order to move Ferdinand from his grief-stricken inertia. As ever, the games come to life because a true understanding of motivation is being newly discovered each time you play.

Whilst maintaining this emotional landscape encourage the children to physically stretch themselves, both as Ariel and Ferdinand. The game provides the opportunity to explore flowing movement, directly combating the stiffness of body the children experience in their daily lives. Use Ferdinand's words 'Where should this music be? I'th'air? Or th'earth?' as an impulse for Ariel to stretch herself high as air and low as earth, creating the impression that her sound is coming from all around him.

When you have practised and repeated the vocal and physical qualities of the game, come back to the circle to share.

How now? Moody?

This game uses the moment Ariel is freed from her pine tree prison by Prospero's magic to make a substantial exploration of facial expressiveness. It is a stand-alone game in terms of the narrative of the play and as such is similar to 'Teaching Caliban to speak'. Both games are set within the play's backstory.

'How now? Moody?' is primarily a game of facial expression, which marks a development from previous games in which techniques of copying, 'throwing' and 'catching' are used to explore different faces. In this game the cues for Ariel's facial expressions are Prospero's words, Prospero himself does not make the faces.

Using the changing rhythm of the heartbeat to express Ariel's imprisoned physicality in the pine tree, the game also provides an opportunity to explore how the body feels when moods change, showing that we are never in 'neutral' but rather our interior rhythms and exterior bodies constantly reflect our changing emotions.

Demonstration

Before playing memorize these lines

Prospero: How now? Moody?
Happy?
Sad?
Angry?
Surprised?
Disgusted?
Afraid?
What is't that you demand?
Ariel: My liberty

Two players are in the circle, facing each other an arm's length apart. One plays Prospero, standing upright with a commanding expression and the other is Ariel trapped in her pine tree. She is sitting on the floor, one hand hugging her knees tight into her body and the other beating out the heartbeat rhythm on her chest, which she continues throughout the whole game. She is looking up to Prospero with a fearful expression. To begin he says:

How now? Moody?

He then begins to name the six 'moods' and as he does her face changes to match each one, trying to please him by obeying his words, all the while maintaining the heartbeats. First he says:

Happy?

Ariel assumes a happy smiling expression, the heartbeat becomes lighter, almost a flutter. She keeps her body locked in her 'pine tree prison' but at the same time she appears to shimmer with happiness.
      After about five seconds Prospero says:

Sad?

Maintaining the rhythm of the heartbeat, her expression immediately changes to sad. Her tempo becomes slower and heavier, her body slumped and gloomy.
      After about five seconds Prospero says:

Angry?

Ariel's heartbeat becomes powerful and thumping, her expression changes to an angry accusative scowl.
      After about five seconds Prospero says:

Surprised?

Ariel assumes the expression of surprise as if it has landed from nowhere, creating an inward gasp of wonder. With each heartbeat she repeats this little gasp of surprise as if it is being re-newed with each breath.
      After about five seconds Prospero says:

Disgusted?

Ariel's expression dissolves in disgust as if she is about to vomit. Her heartbeats become slow and with each one she re-invigorates the 'heaving' action.

After about five seconds Prospero says:

Afraid?

Ariel's heartbeat increasingly picks up pace, her expression is full of fear as if she is about to howl, pleading with him for liberty.

After about five seconds Prospero asks:

What is't that you demand?

Maintaining the heartbeats, Ariel says:

My liberty

After about five seconds Prospero points to her, clicking his fingers and says:

Thou art free.

At this Ariel is released from the pine tree; she leaps up from the floor, creating the POE, jumps high in the air, and lands in front of Prospero, making tiny fluttery heartbeats against her chest as if her heart were beating faster than she can speak, she says:

What shall I do?
Say what?
What shall I do?

She elongates the sound of the word 'Do' both times.

After some breathing space, the players swap roles and play again.

Playing with the children

If the child is completely unable to understand word cues, try basic signing and/or picture cards to stimulate his responses. If the child is struggling use your instructive playfulness, giving the instruction as

Prospero and then immediately showing them the face they need to make. Alternatively elicit the help of another adult or child to play Prospero and pair up with the child as an Ariel duo, they can then copy you whilst you both take your word cues from Prospero.

For children with cognitive understanding use the game to explore and develop how each facial expression makes Ariel – and thereby the child – feel, both on the inside and on the outside. The interior life is expressed through the speed and quality of the heartbeat as it changes with each mood, reflecting the inner rhythm of Ariel's feelings; encourage the children to explore these differences as they play the game, heightening the fast happy beats in contrast to the very slow sad beats giving colour and expressiveness to each one.

Additionally encourage the child to experience each of the changes of mood through their outer physical life, the slump of sadness, the shimmer of the happiness, the tautness of disgust, the sudden alertness of a surprise, the anticipation of the fearful body and the constraint of anger. Though they are apparently motionless, stuck in their pine tree, their hearts and bodies are constantly shifting between 'states of being' reflecting their facial expressions.

The moment that Prospero sets Ariel free is relatively easy to achieve, it gives context to the game, allowing a moment of release and narrative from the more serious endeavour of exploring expression and feeling. You do not have to explore each of the six moods in one session, better to introduce a few at a time and add more in as you play the game thoroughly over a longer period.

When you have repeated the game enough times for one day, come back to the circle to share.

Chapter 9

Miranda and Ferdinand

Might I but through my prison once a day
Behold this maid

(The Tempest, I, ii, 597–8)

Before setting eyes on Ferdinand, Miranda has only seen two men
– her father and the monster Caliban. Having lived on the island
for twelve years since babyhood, everything and everybody she sees
during the play is seen for the first time through her fresh eyes.
For her, the sight of Ferdinand is a miracle. Meanwhile Ferdinand,
believing his own father to be drowned is in a state of soulfulness
when Miranda comes into his vision.

These games further develop the challenges of eye contact, spatial
awareness and sensory attentiveness introduced in part one.

The games

- Lovers' magic trance
- Oh you wonder
- Swords of magic
- I charge thee
- I'll carry your logs awhile

The characters

Miranda
Ferdinand
Prospero
Ariel

The targets

- Making eye contact
- Improving facial expressiveness
- Combating problems of spatial awareness and dyspraxia
- Improving language skills

Lovers' magic trance

Ariel brings Ferdinand to Miranda together for the first time. This is an adaptation of the 'Lovers' trance' from *A Midsummer Night's Dream*, although this version has an increased quality of magic with Ariel as the leader. It can be played as a continuous narrative from 'Ariel's trance' (p. 155).

Before playing memorize this line

At the first sight they have changed eyes

Demonstration

To begin, Ariel and Ferdinand are already in the circle playing 'Ariel's trance'. Ariel is leading Ferdinand, and Ferdinand is following, keeping a hand's width distance between the palm of her hand and his face. This time they play in silence. A third actor is playing Miranda sitting at the side of the circle. Prospero is standing beside her. Maintaining the trance with Ferdinand, Ariel moves to Miranda and places her other hand in front of Miranda's face, immediately 'hypnotizing' her. Ariel slowly moves this second hand upward and Miranda follows, rising up from the floor maintaining an equal distance between hand and face, about a hands-width apart. Both Ferdinand and Miranda are now in Ariel's magnetic power.

Ariel slowly begins to move her hands and her body so that the two lovers follow her around the circle, keeping their eyes fixed to her palms, maintaining an equal distance from her hands at all times. None of them make any physical contact. Ferdinand and Miranda are magnetically pushed and pulled by Ariel's every move, all three players keeping the movements slow, soft and flexible, as if ruled by magic. Neither Ferdinand nor Miranda notice that the other is there as Ariel moves one up whilst she moves the other down, one in front whilst the other is behind, one under the other's body – there is no end to the twisting and turning she experiments with.

After a while Ariel slowly starts to bring her hands together, thus bringing the two lovers nearer and nearer to each other. As she slowly turns her palms toward each other she leads Ferdinand and Miranda's faces closer together until the two lovers finally face each other and make eye contact. At this they breathe in and Ariel darts quickly away. This creates the POE and from the side Prospero speaks his line:

At the first sight they have changed eyes.

The actors take a breathing space, swap roles and demonstrate once more.

Playing with the children

Refer to the 'Lovers' trance' notes in Part I (p. 99) for detailed guidance on playing the 'Trance' game with three people. It is a key game providing the opportunity for the children to explore a smooth, flowing physical language, counteracting the awkward stiffness that they so often experience. When they are playing Ariel encourage the children to explore Ariel's qualities of fire and air. Allow these qualities to affect the child's physicality whilst leading the lovers around the circle. When the lovers 'change eyes' the POE should be as short and intense as possible; encourage the children to explore the sensation of 'changing eyes' placing their eyes inside the eyes of the other!

The addition of Prospero to this game was the idea of a very enthusiastic child, who wanted to be involved at all times. I had mentioned Prospero's line of 'changing eyes' and it was her suggestion that she play him and speak the line at the opportune moment, which she did perfectly every single time. This role in the game has now become standard every time I teach it.

When you have repeated the game a few times, come back to the circle to share.

Oh you wonder

> At the first sight they have changed eyes
>
> (*The Tempest*, I, ii, 529–30)

This is a version of 'Lovestruck' from Part I which includes playing the 'Doyoyoying!' This game explores Miranda and Ferdinand's 'eye changing' moment, picking up the narrative precisely where the last game ended. In this version both players make the 'Doyoyoying!' as opposed to one player (Titania) in *A Midsummer Night's Dream*. The fundamental aim of this game is for the children to explore making eye contact. The eyes themselves are at the centre of the endeavour.

It's fun to teach the 'Doyoyoying!' immediately after the 'Heartbeat hellos' and use it for 'Throwing the face' at the beginning of a session.

Demonstration

Begin by teaching the children the 'Doyoyoying!':

Think cartoon, specifically a cartoon character whose eyes widen and leap out on stalks when falling in love at first sight. Join your thumbs and forefingers together creating two circles; place them to your eyes making 'spectacles' touching your own face. Now stare through the circles and, cartoon style, as if your eyes are bouncing out on stalks exclaim the sound 'Doyoyoying!' while at the same time shaking your 'finger spectacles' a few inches away from your face.

Practise the 'Doyoyoying!' around the circle before continuing with the demonstration.

Before playing memorize these lines

Ferdinand: Oh you wonder
Miranda/Ferdinand: I love you

Two actors are in the circle, one is Miranda, the other Ferdinand. They stand an arm's length away from each other making no eye contact. To start, both players look up and into each other's eyes. On seeing each other, they take an inbreath of delight and together they both make the 'Doyoyoying!' with their face, hands and voice as described above.

Still looking into Miranda's eyes and maintaining an arm's length from her, Ferdinand says:

> Oh you wonder

After a second or two, Miranda sighs deeply, sliding her voice from high to low and turns her eyes away from him, overcome with love.

She keeps her gaze turned away from him, moving her body so that he has to walk around her to find her eyes once more. When he does, they 'change eyes' again by repeating the sequence; beginning with an intake of breath, followed by the 'Doyoyoying'! and Ferdinand's words:

> Oh you wonder

And after a few seconds Miranda sighs and turns away.

The players repeat the sequence twice more and the final time, Miranda does not turn away, but remains looking into Ferdinand's eyes and speaking in unison, taking a breath between each word they say:

> I ... love ... you

This provides the POE. The players take some breathing space, swap roles and play again.

Playing with the children

If you have not played 'Lovestruck' before it is essential to read through the guidance for all four stages in Part I (p. 33), which give you the option to break the game down into easy phases, if necessary. All the advice is applicable, simply replace Titania and Bottom with Ferdinand and Miranda and change the text accordingly.

Adopt a heightened playing style to encourage the children to find the lightheartedness in the sighing of Miranda. There is, however, a balance to be struck, it is essential that you act well – always finding the truth of the moment and not being tempted to comment or satirize in any way. Think of a heightened playing style as meaning 'intensified truth'. Every child and actor who plays this game seems to find an idiosyncratic way of expressing first love, with varying tempos and gestures, all of which should be encouraged.

Photo 14 The 'Doyoyoying!' with two people (photo © Nick Spratling)

Whilst you are playing with a child, maintain the freshness with which the lovers 'change eyes' and ensure that every time you make the 'Doyoyoying!' it is as if it is happening for the first time. To be present in the moment is one of the all-time great notes for an actor and essential when playing these games with the children. Ensure that eye contact has been made whilst you play one on one with the child and when you have repeated the game a few times, come back to the circle to share.

Swords of magic

> Too light winning
> Makes the prize light
>
> (*The Tempest*, I, ii, 544–5)

Prospero secretly approves of the match between his daughter and Ferdinand, but he intends to put Ferdinand to the test before he grants him her hand.

This game, played by Prospero and Ferdinand, is a version of the 'Invisible swords' game from Part I, using the same physical framework and aiming to challenge the children's spatial awareness and physical co-ordination whilst encouraging eye contact and language skills.

Demonstration

Before playing memorize these lines

Prospero: No! No! No!
Ferdinand: Yes! Yes! Yes!

Two actors are in the circle, playing Prospero and Ferdinand, standing about five or six feet apart; they maintain this distance between each other for the whole game and never make any physical contact. Prospero assumes his commanding expression and Ferdinand assumes a face of frustration. They make eye contact and stretch their arms out in front of their bodies, hands clasped together as if holding invisible swords, knees slightly bent, preparing to spring into action. To play they will take turns as striker and receiver. (There should be enough room for the striker to swing his invisible sword from left to right in front of his body without touching the receiver.)

To begin Prospero becomes the striker, and maintaining his distance from Ferdinand, he swings his invisible sword from right to left aiming toward Ferdinand's head saying 'No!' Ferdinand ducks down and pops back up in response to the strike as if the sword has gone over his body. Prospero waits for them both to settle and makes eye contact with Ferdinand before the next swing. Next Prospero takes a second swing from right to left, saying 'No!' as he aims toward Ferdinand's feet, who responds by jumping up as if dodging the sword. Ferdinand jumps as high as he can, knees bent up underneath him. After this, both players take time to settle again and make eye contact. Finally Prospero makes a stab with his invisible sword toward Ferdinand's tummy saying 'No!' and Ferdinand responds with a leap backward to dodge the tummy blow. This is the end of the first round. There are always three strikes in this order for one player's turn.

Now the actors swap roles, Ferdinand becomes the striker, Prospero the receiver and they repeat the exercise. When Ferdinand is the striker he says 'Yes!' with every strike he makes. The actors should swap round three times in order for the children to learn the game.

A variation of the game, which adds the next level of difficulty, is for the striker to strike the head, feet or tummy in any order he chooses. Removing the comfort of the known order of play requires a higher level of concentration from both players. Played in this way the settling moment of eye contact between each strike becomes crucial.

Playing with the children

Read and use the guidance for 'Invisible swords' in Part I (p. 103) if you are new to this game. Many children initially find it difficult to add text and, although I have included the simple use of 'Yes!' and 'No!' in this demonstration, you may find that children initially need to play without words to allow for total concentration of their physical co-ordination. If they are still struggling when you add the words, play with them as a duo allowing them to copy you and giving them support in practising the skill of speaking and moving at the same time. Ensure that you are working with the child at their own pace and not missing out any of the necessary steps in order to get a 'final result'; playing each phase of the game itself is result enough.

Encourage children who can manage the physical and vocal co-ordination to embody the distinct characteristics of Prospero and Ferdinand; the more commanding Prospero becomes the more frustrated it makes Ferdinand and conversely as Ferdinand's frustration increases Prospero enjoys his commanding status. When you have repeated the game several times, come back to the circle to share.

Adding words.

The game is played exactly as before, with two additional lines of text to stretch the children's speech and language skills.

Demonstration

Before playing memorize these lines

Prospero: Sea water shalt thou drink
Ferdinand: No, as I am a man

Two actors are in the circle, five or six feet apart, playing Prospero and Ferdinand. Arms stretched out in front of them, they are ready with their invisible double-handed swords, knees slightly bent, preparing to spring into action. For this demonstration the striker uses the original order; first head, then feet and then tummy and the receiver responds accordingly with ducking, jumping and leaping back. The first striker is Prospero who speaks his line, using the natural rhythm for the words and the 'strikes of the sword' to fit together, striking and speaking at the same time, in bold type here for guidance.

Sea **water shalt** thou **drink**

He makes his three strikes and Ferdinand ducks, jumps and leaps back accordingly. Ferdinand then proceeds to make his three strikes, speaking his words:

No, **as I am** a **man**

and Prospero ducks, jumps and leaps back accordingly.

After a little breathing space, the actors swap roles and play again.

Playing with the children

Encourage the children to experience the physical forcefulness of the sword-fighting game whilst they are making sounds, so that the body and voice are engaged together in the effort to communicate. If a child struggles with combining the physical game with the language but is really keen to have a try, allow them the opportunity to copy your voice, it doesn't matter what the outcome sounds like. This may be the only opportunity for the child to practise making new sounds and shapes with his mouth and vocal cords and it is only through practice that he will make any progress.

When you have challenged the child's vocal skills to their limits, whilst repeating the game a few times come back to the circle to share.

I charge thee

Prospero uses his magic to further frustrate and control Ferdinand as Ferdinand continues to try to fight him.

This game develops the physical relationship between the two players, challenging the children's spatial awareness, role-playing abilities and language skills.

Demonstration

Before playing memorize these lines

Prospero:	I charge thee
	Follow me
Ferdinand:	No!
	Might I but through my prison once a day
	Behold this maid
Prospero:	I'll manacle thy feet and legs together

Two players are in the circle. One is Prospero and the other Ferdinand. They stand facing one another a few paces apart. They are making eye contact. To begin Prospero points both hands at Ferdinand casting his first spell, he keeps his hands in this 'taser' position and speaks:

I charge thee

Ferdinand immediately tries to say the word' No!', but freezes, as if paralyzed by Prospero. His eyes are locked into Prospero's gaze. He continues to make huge effort to move and speak as if pushing against an invisible wall but he can't make any progress. After a few seconds, Prospero drops his hands to his sides and thereby releases Ferdinand from the spell.

Before Ferdinand can move again Prospero raises his hands to the sides of his head, casting his second spell. He speaks:

I charge thee

Again Ferdinand immediately tries to say 'No!' This time his feet have been frozen to the ground, his eyes are locked to the eyes of Prospero, but the rest of his body can move. Ferdinand uses all his energy, swinging his arms and body toward Prospero but unable to make any progress forward. He tries in vain to reach him whilst also trying to say 'No!' but unable to do either. After a few seconds Prospero drops his hands to his sides and thereby releases Ferdinand from the spell. Ferdinand is exhausted with the effort.

Prospero then alternates between these two spells, each time using the words 'I charge thee'; putting his hands forward to make Ferdinand completely freeze and hands up to make Ferdinand swing his arms. He and Ferdinand both take a breath in between each spell.

After three or four turns, Prospero casts his third spell. He points one arm out at full stretch toward Ferdinand and begins to slowly move it down toward the ground, saying:

Follow

Ferdinand's eyes are immediately transfixed to the pointed finger of Prospero. He follows it until he is kneeling on the floor as if in prayer.

Ferdinand still staring at Prospero's finger, speaks:

Might I but through my prison once a day
Behold this maid

To finish the game Prospero stands and casts his last spell over Ferdinand. He speaks:

I'll manacle thy feet and legs together

Ferdinand cries out:

No!

And he bends his body further forward, crossing his legs and so that his head meets his feet.

After some breathing space, the actors swap roles and play again.

Playing with the children

Break the game down to four simple stages if necessary, exploring each stage as a separate spell that Ferdinand endures. The heart of the game lies in the first two spells which provide an opportunity for the children playing Ferdinand to physically engage with their bodies by pretending to be paralyzed, thereby actively using all their muscle power and yet not getting anywhere. The effect should be exhausting and cathartic. Encourage the children to push against 'invisible air or water' and if they find this difficult to comprehend allow them to push against your own body for a while to get the idea of the physical engagement. The game begins to work when the child playing Ferdinand goes on a physical journey and becomes worn down by Prospero.

The third and fourth spells are easier to achieve, allowing the children an opportunity to engage with the language and embody the images. Modify these two spells to suit the children's cognition, speaking the words yourself if necessary.

You can play this game sitting, standing, or on the move. To play on the move use a version of the 'Shadow' game with Ferdinand following Prospero. Prospero can turn round at any time, saying 'I charge thee', either with his arms forward or arms up thereby putting a different spell on Ferdinand each time. When Prospero has had enough, he can turn round a final time saying 'Follow' and the two players play the game to its end.

When you have repeated the game and the children have played both parts come back to the circle to share.

I'll carry your logs awhile

Prospero makes Ferdinand carry a thousand logs from one end of the island to the other; meanwhile Miranda secretly comes to help him.

'I'll carry your logs awhile' develops the previous game's challenge of physically engaging the body whilst introducing a sensory understanding of the difference between lightness and weight.

Demonstration

Before playing memorize these lines

Ferdinand: I must remove a thousand logs
        And carry them to this pile
Miranda: I'll bear your logs a while
        I'll carry them to the pile

I'll be your wife if you'll have me
Ferdinand: Here's my hand
Miranda: And mine, with my heart in't.

Two players are in the circle. One is Ferdinand and the other is Miranda. Miranda stands directly behind Ferdinand an arm's length away. Ferdinand bends his knees deeply and holds his arms out in front of him as if carrying unbearably heavy logs, his body shape is low and heavy. In complete contrast Miranda's body shape is high and light as if in an ecstasy of secret love.

To begin Ferdinand begins to slowly make his way around the circle, getting lower and heavier with each step he takes as if the hefty weight of the logs is going to topple him over. As he moves Miranda follows him, staying close behind, silently dancing and leaping for joy, as if she were light as a feather. Her dancing is secretive as if she doesn't want him to see her feelings.

The contrasting movements of the two players remain in complete opposition for the duration of the game. Ferdinand makes his way around the circle taking deep breaths. He speaks as slowly and heavily as possible:

I must remove a thousand logs
And carry them to this pile

Miranda now moves to the front of Ferdinand, holds out her arms and in one movement she 'takes the logs'. At this moment they swap their body shape: Miranda's knees drop forcibly into a deep bend with the weight of the imaginary logs, her whole body low and heavy whilst Ferdinand leaps into the air, his body shape and movements high and light, moving behind Miranda and dancing with the secret joy of love. This impulsive swapping moment provides the POE. Now Miranda continues the slow heavy journey with Ferdinand secretly dancing lightly behind her. She breathes deeply and speaks slowly:

I'll bear your logs a while
I'll carry them to the pile

After a few paces Ferdinand moves to the front of Miranda, holds out his arms and 'takes the logs'. Again they swap body shapes,

Photo 15 I must remove a thousand logs (photo © Jirye Lee)

Photo 16 Demonstrating the game (photo © Jirye Lee)

Ferdinand immediately resuming the heaviness and Miranda immediately resuming the lightness.

They play two more rounds in this way, speaking their lines as they carry the imaginary logs and maintaining the contrast between heavy and light. On the third round instead of swapping the logs, both players stretch their arms out as if to drop the logs to the floor. They fall to their knees in front of each other, making direct eye contact.

Miranda speaks:

I'll be your wife if you'll have me

Ferdinand holds out his hand, speaking:

Here's my hand

Miranda responds by offering her hand to him, speaking:

And mine, with my heart in't.

They clasp each other's hands providing a final POE.

After some breathing space the players swap roles and play again.

Playing with the children

Ensure that the children genuinely share the moment of 'swapping' to the best of their ability. If they 'take the logs' encourage them to physically drop down low allowing their voices, faces and bodies to register the heavy effort before beginning to move around the circle. Conversely if they 'give the logs' encourage them to feel as light as they can, immediately springing up with bounce and speed.

Be expressive and individual in your own interpretations and encourage the children to be the same, your generosity will pay dividends for the child. This game is particularly popular and was originally developed with the children taking part in the research project in Ohio. I vividly remember one child blowing kisses and miming a silent fluttery heartbeat as she played Miranda. When it was her turn to carry the logs she found it very hard to bend her knees and seemed to fold herself in half almost touching her toes in order to drag her imaginary logs along the ground, creating a

Photo 17 I'll bear your logs a while

Photo 18 Here's my hand

Photo 19 And mine with my heart in't

perfect contrast between the two states of being. She couldn't do exactly what the actor had done, but took his version of the game, especially the kisses and the flutters, and made them her own. Her speech and language was very low – she also wore a hearing aid – but she had the rhythm of the words in her head and would appropriate the sounds to the beat of the line. It was beautiful to watch how she adapted the game for herself, copying the actor she played with and then giving it her own interpretation.

When you have repeated the game a few times come back to the circle to share.

Chapter 10

The clowns

Hast thou not dropped from heaven?
Out of the moon I do assure thee. I was the man i' th' moon when time was.

(The Tempest, II, ii, 142–4)

The jester Trinculo and the butler Stephano have been shipwrecked on the island both thinking the other is dead. They meet Caliban who believes they have dropped from heaven and asks them to help him kill Prospero.

The humour of the clowns sets up a comic vein within which these games develop the children's eye focus and sensory impulses. The chapter culminates with a 'falling' game, which encourages the children's sense of trust.

The games

- Fearful and disgusted
- Double take
- A monster of the isle
- The falling game

The characters

- Trinculo
- Stephano
- Caliban
- Ariel
- Prospero

The targets

- Facial recognition and expressiveness
- Development of eye focus
- Sensory awareness
- The impulse to speak
- Introduction of trust and responsibility
- Development of spatial awareness

Fearful and disgusted

Trinculo is fearful; alone on the island, consumed with his fear of the storm, whilst Stephano is disgusted; drinking to comfort himself. The characters are introduced using the familiar structure of 'Throwing the face, body and voice'. You can also introduce the characters using a simpler version sitting down around the circle to begin with. In this way the fearful and disgusted expressions can be incorporated into 'Throwing the face' at the beginning of your session.

Demonstration/playing with the children

Before playing memorize these lines

Trinculo: Alas, the storm is come again
          I know not where to hide my head
Stephano   I shall no more to sea to sea
          Here shall I die alone

Introducing Trinculo

Everyone stands up around the circle, prepared to use their faces, bodies and voices. An actor assumes the fearful face and body shape of Trinculo, his legs, feet and arms wobble and shake with fearful energy, hands fluttering and eyes looking skyward as if afraid of the on-coming storm.

A second actor on the opposite side of the room prepares to become the 'catcher'. Once Trinculo and the catcher are ready, give the instruction of '1, 2, 3 Throw' at which Trinculo using a fearful voice speaks:

Photo 20 Trinculo's fearful face (photo © Jirye Lee)

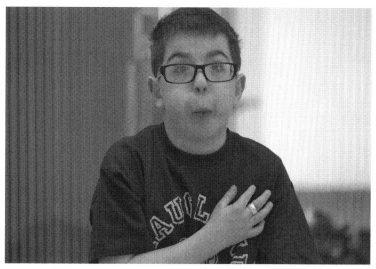

Photo 21 Stephano's disgusted face (photo © Jirye Lee)

> Alas, the storm is come again
> I know not where to hide my head

and immediately 'throws' his fearful face and body shape across the circle, jumping a little off the ground with the effort, and the catcher 'catches' it, immediately shaking with fear, with his eyes looking skyward. He takes a breath and brings Trinculo further to life speaking his words.

> Alas, the storm is come again
> I know not where to hide my head

Use the same instruction of '1, 2, 3 Throw' to play the game with the whole group around the circle, always ensuring that thrower and catcher are ready and making eye contact before they play, speaking the words once they have 'caught' the body. Vary the choice of catchers using pairs, small groups and sometimes the whole group to bring the fearful jester to life; by the end of the round the trembling body and voice of Trinculo is embedded in the children's bodies and minds.

Introducing Stephano

Now introduce Stephano. The disgusted face is used to bring his drunkenness to life, as if he is just about to be sick.

An actor assumes the disgusted face and body shape of Stephano, he is unbalanced as if waves of disgust are convulsing his body, seasick, drunk and disgusted at himself. A second actor on the opposite side of the room prepares to become the 'catcher'. Once Stephano and the catcher are ready, give the instruction of '1, 2, 3 Throw' at which Stephano begins to speak using the disgusted expression to colour his voice:

> I shall no more to sea to sea
> Here shall I die alone

The actor adds in hiccups and burps if he wishes and immediately 'throws' his disgusted face and body shape across the circle, jumping a little off the ground with the effort, and the catcher 'catches' it, immediately convulsed with disgust, and trying not to be sick. He

Photo 22 Ready to throw the face (photo © Jirye Lee)

Photo 23 The throw! (photo © Jirye Lee)

takes a breath and brings Stephano further to life speaking the words.

> I shall no more to sea to sea
> Here shall I die alone

Use the same instruction of '1, 2, 3 Throw' to play the game with the whole group around the circle, always ensuring that thrower and catcher are ready and making eye contact before they play, speaking the words once they have 'caught' the body. Vary the choice of catchers using pairs, small groups and sometimes the whole group to bring the drunken shipwrecked butler to life; by the end of the round the disgusted body and voice of Stephano should be embedded in the children's bodies and minds.

Split into pairs and small groups to play if you think the children will benefit from exploring the characters with one on one attention. However if you have thrown the bodies and voices around the circle sufficiently, and you feel that the characters of Trinculo and Stephano are sufficiently embedded in the children's bodies, move on to the next stage.

The game

Once the characters have been introduced the game involves one player changing back and forth between fearful and disgusted on the instruction of their partner.

Demonstration

Two players are in the circle. One is the clown and the other the leader. They stand a few feet apart and make eye contact. To begin the leader says 'Disgusted' at which point the clown immediately assumes the face, body and voice of Stephano and speaks his words, fully embodying the character:

> I shall no more to sea to sea
> Here shall I die alone

The leader then says 'Fearful' at which point the clown immediately assumes the face, body and voice of Trinculo and speaks his words fully embodying the character:

Alas, the storm is come again
I know not where to hide my head

Now the leader can choose which instruction to give. He may change the clown's role once more saying 'Disgusted' at which the clown becomes Stephano again. Alternatively the leader can say 'More fearful' or 'More disgusted' at which the clown repeats whichever role he is in, increasing the intensity of emotion – either fear or disgust. The leader varies the instructions until the clown has repeated both roles several times.

After some breathing space the actors swap roles and play again.

Playing with the children

The heart of the game is to develop expressiveness in the children's faces, bodies and voices. Use the alternating instructions to provide an opportunity for the children to become more flexible and playful. It's useful to think of the act of 'playing' as 'changing'; to play is to change. This game therefore has playfulness right at its core. Each POE is found in the moment another change is made.

When the child is your leader, take this note to heart and embody the changes as completely as possible, ensuring that you listen hard for each of their instructions. As ever, you may find yourself prompting them to give you an instruction and then acting on that instruction, if they need your help in this way be ready and willing to give it.

Its fun to stick on one expression for four or five goes, ensuring that the children increase their emotion with each instruction given. For example if you say 'Fearful, fearful ... more fearful, even more fearful ... really really really fearful' it is then a wonderful relief for them to be able to change to disgusted! Be sure that you are as inventive as possible with your instructions allowing the children to lose their inhibitions.

When you have repeated the game and played both parts come back to the circle to share.

Double take

Caliban is hiding from his tormenting spirits; he lies flat on the ground under a tarpaulin, feet and head sticking out of either end. Trinculo is escaping the storm, trying to find somewhere to hide. He sees Caliban, and looks at him with disbelief. This game focuses on that moment.

The game gives the children the opportunity to explore the skill of focused looking, challenging the children's habits wherein maintaining eye focus can be an intense struggle. Trinculo plays the game alone, using a cartoon style similar to the 'Doyoyoying!', whilst Caliban lies on the floor.

At the end of the game with the storm breaking once more, Trinculo gets under the tarpaulin with him. I did try using sleeping bags once to represent the tarpaulin, breaking my own rule of never using props but they were a hindrance rather than an asset – in this game Caliban and Trinculo simply lie flat on the ground, face down, hands covering their heads; bodies and voices are all you need.

Demonstration/playing with the children

Teach the 'Double take' to the children around the circle. One actor sitting down, can demonstrate.

THE DOUBLE TAKE SEQUENCE

Think cartoon. Begin by looking down at a spot on the floor in front of you about two feet away. Open your eyes wide with a surprised expression as if you have seen Caliban the monster.

Breathing in, look away to the side for a second or two as if in disbelief and then, breathing out, quickly look straight back to the same spot to check what you saw was true.

After a couple of seconds of staring at the spot, repeat the action:

Breathing in, look away to the side for a second or two and then, breathing out, quickly look straight back to the same spot.

After a couple more seconds of staring at the spot repeat the action once more:

Breathing in, look away to the side for a second or two but this time when you come back to looking at the same spot make an exaggerated 'looking' movement by scooping your chin down and up as if to stare better and closer, making a cartoon dog like 'Harumph' sound. (This is based on Scooby-Doo and originated with the actors on the research team in Ohio.)

Now breathe in deeply through your nose as if to smell the monster, leaning your head back, eyes looking away from the floor.

Finally, keep your head back and just moving your eyes, look down to the spot once more. After a couple of seconds of looking, make a cartoon-style speeded-up shake of your eyes and face as if in disbelief and fear. Your lips shake as a result of the movement and your voice makes a quiet high-pitched sound. This provides the POE.

The whole sequence lasts no more than ten seconds.

Once you have demonstrated the sequence, practise the 'Double take' around the circle together in unison. It is good fun to create a collective rhythm at the end in which everybody is shaking their 'speeded up' eyes faces and lips. You do not have to spend too long teaching in unison as it is more beneficial to teach this game one to one.

PLAYING WITHOUT WORDS

Two actors are in the circle. One is Caliban lying face down on the floor and the other is Trinculo, standing an arm's length away from Caliban but not looking at him. Trinculo assumes his fearful expression. He looks down to Caliban and on seeing him he acts out the 'Double take' sequence from beginning to end. He makes each phase completely clear and precise, finishing with the speedy 'face-shake' creating the POE.

When he has finished the players take a breathing space, swap roles and play again.

Playing with the children

To begin, sit down opposite the child to teach and practise the sequence, taking your time not to hurry each phase. Initially play the game with both of you looking at the same spot on the floor, creating an enjoyable rhythm between the two of you. Develop your own version of the cartoon 'Scooby-Doo harumph' and the final speedy 'face shake' within the natural flowing rhythm of the game and encourage the child to do the same. Have fun.

Once you have explored this version, try making eye contact with each other in replacement of looking at a spot on the floor. Everything else remains the same. Ensure that the child is familiar with the rhythm of the game so that the extra challenge of making eye contact remains enjoyable. Try this version a couple of times, giving lots of praise if they make consistent eye contact.

Finally, practise the game up on your feet with the child, allowing them to lie down as Caliban while you play Trinculo and vice versa. It's important that the children feel they are sharing the games with you, and that you are truly enjoying yourself. The beneficial side of the work is embedded deep in the games and begins to take root through a shared pleasurable experience. If you are working with a small group, allow the children to lie down together as Caliban or conversely encourage them to make a small chorus of fearful Trinculos keeping the rhythm of the sequence tight together.

Ensure that they work through each phase of the sequence as Trinculo; even if it means you have to give them encouragement from your position as the face-down Caliban, your instructive playfulness is useful here.

When you have repeated the game several times and the child has played both roles, come back to the circle to share.

Adding words

The words fit perfectly with the sequence, which itself remains exactly the same.

Demonstration

Before playing memorize these lines

Trinculo: What have we here?
A man or a fish?
Dead or alive?
A fish, he smells like a fish

Exactly as before, two actors are in the circle. One is Caliban lying face down on the floor, hands covering his head and the other is Trinculo, standing an arm's length away from Caliban but not looking at him. Trinculo assumes his fearful expression.

To begin, Trinculo looks down to Caliban, his eyes widen and he says:

What have we here?

Photo 24 A fish, he smells like a fish (photo © Jirye Lee)

Breathing in, he looks away to the side for a second or two as if in disbelief and then, breathing out, quickly looks straight back to the same spot to check what he saw was true. He then says:

A man or a fish?

Breathing in, he looks away to the side for a second or two in even greater disbelief and then, breathing out, quickly looks straight back to the same spot to check what he saw was true. He then says:

Dead or alive?

Breathing in, again he looks away to the side for a second or two and then, breathing out, he makes an exaggerated 'looking' movement with a scoop of his chin as if to stare better and closer, making a 'Harumph' sound like Scooby-Doo. He then says:

A fish!

Now he breathes in deeply through his nose as if to smell the fish smell of Caliban, leaning his head back and eyes looking away from the floor. He speaks as if he can't breathe:

He smells like a fish

Finally he looks back down to the spot once more and seeing Caliban he breathes out and makes the speeded-up cartoon-style shake of his face, eyes and lips. This provides the POE.

The two players take some breathing space, swap roles and play again.

Playing with the children

The addition of words always needs to be taken slowly, ensuring that everything the child has achieved in the soundless version of the game remains intact once language is introduced. The breathing is particularly helpful in this game and is worth considering although as a rule you should refrain from giving the children 'breathing instructions' as it is likely to make them self-conscious and anxious. You should of course be aware of their breathing and their state of relaxation whilst you are playing; some children do have a tendency of holding their breath in and trying to speak at the same time.

If this is the case use this game to explore breathing as an intrinsic part of acting for example in this scenario – the breath out expresses Trinculo's disbelief. Encourage the child to deliberately breathe out at the end of each stage before they speak, using a short puff of air to enhance Trinculo's incredulity and add to the comedy. If the children are struggling, try a version where they breathe out and you say the words to begin with, allowing them to add the words in when they feel they can. If the child focuses on their breathing, speaking the words becomes much easier.

If you find that exploring breathing in this way – making it an integral part of a character's mood – is particularly beneficial and enjoyable for the child then add it to your techniques of playing as you build up your own ways of using the games.

When you have repeated and practised the game, come back to the circle to share.

Adding an ending

This ending adds a narrative through-line to the story, heightening the children's sensory awareness. The entire stimulus for Trinculo's fear in the game so far has involved sight and looking, now his fear is stimulated by sound – the noise of the on-coming storm. Ensure that the sound of the storm is made as sensitively as needs be. Create a way of banging on the floor that is surprising for Trinculo but not alarming for the children. If necessary warn the children that the storm sound will be made and practise it beforehand.

Demonstration

Two players are in the circle, Caliban lying on the ground and Trinculo an arm's length away from him; he acts out the 'Double take' all the way through. At the end, three or four actors bang the floor softly with the flats of their hands, making the noise of the storm. Trinculo hears this and 'jumps out of his skin' with fright. He looks up and says his lines:

> Alas the storm is come again
> I know not where to hide my head

And he quickly joins Caliban, lying head to toe on the floor.
    The two actors swap roles and play the scene again.

Playing with the children

Encourage the children's sensory awareness, clearly defining the difference between Trinculo's slow responses when he looks at Caliban during the 'Double take' and his fast 'jumpy' response when he hears the storm. The noise has the effect of waking him up to his fearful predicament, causing him to 'jump out of his skin'. This is a useful phrase to explain to the children and plays a central part in the next game when Stephano is added to the story.
    When you have repeated the game all the way through a few times come back to the circle to share.

A monster of the isle

Stephano, drunk and alone, stumbles upon the shape of Caliban and Trinculo lying top to toe on the ground. He mistakes them for a four-legged monster with two voices. This game requires all three players to take an active role and has a distinctive comic rhythm embedded within it. The game continues the exploration of sensory impulse, defining the difference between vision and hearing and providing an intense listening experience for all three players.

Demonstration

WITHOUT WORDS

This first stage is played using the sounds 'OH' and 'HA'.
Before playing memorize this

Stephano:	OH!
Caliban:	OH!
Trinculo:	OH!
Stephano:	HA!

Three players are in the circle. Caliban and Trinculo are lying face down on the ground, head to toe, Caliban's head next to Trinculo's feet and Trinculo's feet next to Caliban's head.

Stephano stands an arm's length away. He assumes his drunken disgusted face and body shape.

To begin he looks at the Caliban/Trinculo shape, he counts the four legs and with a surprised expression he says:

OH!

Caliban hears this, and in response he raises his head up.
With a surprised, fearful expression Caliban says:

OH!

Caliban places his head back down on the floor.
Trinculo raises his head and with a surprised expression he says:

OH!

Trinculo places his head back down on the floor.
Stephano jumps out of his skin in response to this second voice, saying:

HA!

This provides the POE.
The sequence takes no longer than five–ten seconds.

The players immediately begin again, repeating the sequence three times. With each 'OH!' and 'HA!' their collective sense of fear and surprise increases.

They take a breathing space, swap roles and play the game again.

Playing with the children

Play in groups of no less than three. If playing with more, double up the characters, ensuring that each child gets the chance to play each part. The game makes clear requirements on each player; Caliban and Trinculo respond only to the sound of the voices, meanwhile Stephano responds to what he hears and sees and all the three players share an intense listening silence between them.

Many of the children speak with a flat tone of voice that does not register their emotions, leading them to become increasingly frustrated at not having their feelings understood. The game directly challenges this vocal flatness and is entirely focused on allowing the pure sound of the voice to change and develop in tone and register, providing a humorous and pleasurable opportunity for the children to practise their expressiveness.

Encourage the children to explore the difference between Stephano's two sounds. His first is a surprised sound – 'OH!' and his second is a palpably different shocked sound – 'HA!' as he 'jumps out of his skin' at the unexpected sound of Trinculo's voice.

Practise the game, ensuring that the children change their vocal expressiveness from surprised to shock using the exercise to develop their vocal range, increasing their expressiveness each time they speak.

Meanwhile when the children play Caliban and Trinculo on the floor ensure that they increase their vocal fear and surprise with each round of the game and that, as far as possible, their sounds are always connected to their feelings. Encourage them to be as attentive as possible, lifting their heads, speaking with feeling, and placing their heads back down again, their heads rising and falling each time they say 'OH', producing a comic effect. It's possible for them to play with their eyes closed to increase sensory awareness.

The game has a fast, natural speed of playing but make sure that you practise it slowly at first, exploring every nuance of the exercise. When each child has had a turn with all the parts, come back to the circle to share.

Adding words.

This version has exactly the same framework as before with the text replacing the sounds, challenging the children's speech and language skills, and developing more humour within the game.

Demonstration

Before playing memorize these lines

Stephano:	A monster of the isle with four legs
Caliban	The spirit torments me
Trinculo:	I know that voice
Stephano:	Ha! Four legs, Two voices!

Begin exactly as before, three players in the circle, Caliban and Trinculo lying head to toe on the ground, Caliban's head next to Trinculo's feet and Trinculo's feet next to Caliban's head.

Stephano stands an arm's length away. He assumes his drunken disgusted face and body shape.

To begin he looks at the Caliban/Trinculo shape. He counts the four legs and with a surprised expression he says:

A monster of the isle with four legs

Caliban hears this, and in response he raises his head up.

With a surprised, fearful expression Caliban says:

The spirit torments me

Caliban places his head back down on the floor.

Trinculo raises his head and with a surprised expression he says:

I know that voice

Trinculo places his head back down on the floor.

Stephano jumps out of his skin in response to the second voice. Stephano says:

Ha! Four legs, Two voices!

This provides the POE.

The sequence takes no longer than five–ten seconds.

The players begin again, repeating the sequence three times. Each time they speak, their collective sense of fear and surprise increases.

They take a breathing space, swap roles and play the game again.

Playing with the children

Ensure that none of the children's sensory and vocal achievements get lost with the addition of the text and that the shared listening silence is present when you practise. The language adds an extra dimension of humour to the game, an element of this work worth reflecting upon. A few years back I was playing these games with a group of teenage boys whose teachers found the demonstrations very amusing, laughing every time they saw Stephano's shock at the two voices. The whole scene tickled them. One of the boys perplexed by their laughter but wanting to join in, asked 'Is this funny?' 'Yes' I answered, to which he said 'Shall I laugh now?' 'Of course, if you like' I replied to which he answered in a slow measured inexpressive tone 'Ha … Ha … Ha' with no intonation or obvious connection to a sense of humour, but trying as hard as he could to have the appropriate response.

At my regular special school I begin the day playing with a class of children who have diverse special needs, some in wheelchairs, some with Down's syndrome, all with complex learning difficulties but none with autism. These sessions are remarkable for the amount of plentiful, infectious laughter the games generate. Immediately after this first session, I teach exactly the same games to a class of children with autism and in place of the guaranteed laughter there is silence, a piercing absence of humour punctuated by hollow laughs wherein some of the children attempt to imitate the adults. At the same time the children experience intense, palpable pleasure playing the games and although the outward show of instinctive laughter is missing, it's clear that the desire to experience it is not.

Use these games of Trinculo and Stephano to encourage the children to experience the humour of the play. Their laughter is likely to be a new and unfamiliar 'skill'. When you have practised and repeated the game several times come back to the circle to share.

The falling game

> Swear how thou escapedst?
> Swum ashore man, like a duck
>
> ...
>
> Though thou canst swim like a duck, thou art made like a goose.
>
> (*The Tempest*, II, ii, 131–136)

Stephano and Trinculo are re-united, and Caliban, who believes they have dropped from heaven, asks them to kill Prospero.

At the heart of the game is a falling experience, requiring a higher level of physical trust than previous games have called for. Trinculo falls forward and back between Stephano and Caliban like an upside down pendulum, creating a mesmeric physical rhythm to the game. With each moment of falling, Trinculo has a momentary experience of weightlessness before being safely caught by the players on either side of him.

Demonstration

Before playing memorize these lines

Trinculo:	Stephano! It's Trinculo!
Stephano:	Trinculo! It's Stephano!
Caliban:	Have you not dropped from heaven?
	Kill my master

Three actors are in the circle, Trinculo between Stephano and Caliban, each an arm's length away from each other. To begin, Trinculo is facing Stephano, with Caliban directly behind him. Caliban and Stephano stretch their arms out in front of them, elbows slightly bent and palms vertical, bracing their hands, arms and bodies to take the weight of the 'falling' Trinculo.

Trinculo, feet together, stands as upright as possible, straight as an arrow from the top of his head down to his heels. He maintains this upright stance all the way through the game, rocking forward and backward on his feet between Stephano and Caliban, like a swinging pendulum.

The falling sequence

To begin the sequence, Trinculo stretches his arms out in front of him, leans forward slightly and presses his palms to the palms of Stephano, who begins to takes his weight.

Trinculo leans forward toward Stephano. He speaks:

> Stephano! It's Trinculo!

Stephano leans back and takes Trinculo's weight. He speaks:

> Trinculo! It's Stephano!

Stephano gently pushes Trinculo away.

Stephano makes an upward swing of his arms when he says Stephano as if celebrating the reconciliation. In one smooth movement he brings his arms back to their starting point, stretched out in front of him, elbows slightly bent and palms vertical, ready to catch again.

Trinculo tips backward toward Caliban.

Here is the first falling moment – backward – providing the POE.

Caliban's hands make contact with Trinculo's back.

Caliban leans back, taking Trinculo's weight. He speaks:

> Have you not dropped from heaven?

Caliban gently pushes Trinculo away.

Caliban makes an upward swing of his arms when he says 'Heaven' as if celebrating the joy of meeting the clowns. In one smooth movement he brings his arms back to their starting point, stretched out in front of him, elbows slightly bent and palms vertical, ready to catch him again.

Trinculo tips forward toward Stephano.

Here is his second falling moment – forward – providing the second POE.

Trinculo places his hands in front of him as he falls forward. He places them palm to palm with Stephano and the sequence begins again.

They repeat the sequence three times, increasing their emotions with each round.

At the last round Caliban says:

Photo 25 To begin (photo © Jirye Lee)

Photo 26 Falling forward (photo © Jirye Lee)

Photo 27 Falling back (photo © Jirye Lee)

Have you not dropped from heaven?

He keeps Trinculo leaning back against him and says:

Kill my master

All three players take an in-breath of surprise and Trinculo jumps up into the middle as if shocked by the request.

After some breathing space, the actors swap roles and play again.

Playing with the children

Ensure that the aim of the game – introducing physical contact and trust into the relationship between players – is the focus of your endeavour. Begin by taking time to practise and engage the children with the falling technique, which involves a combination of physical stability and flexibility. Encourage them to develop a stable upright stance, whilst simultaneously rocking forwards and backwards on their feet. Practise this rocking movement in small degrees, so that no catching is needed at first and the children have time to acclimatize themselves to the new sensation. When you add in the catchers, ensure that they initially keep their hands in contact with the 'faller', removing them inch by inch as everyone becomes confident through practice and repetition.

Allow the moment of weightlessness to develop naturally by approaching the game with these building blocks. Once the falling has begun to take shape, follow this by teaching and practising the game without words. Ensure that the two 'outside' players are trustworthy or add another adult to the team to monitor the catching if you feel the need. The focus of the game is the experience of falling for the central player, but this is no less important than the experience of responsibility that comes with the catchers. Encourage the children to understand that it takes all three people to develop and experience the sensation of trust within the game and ensure that all the children have a turn in the middle as well as playing one of the catchers.

Before adding the language allow the children to engage vocally with pure sound, using 'OH's and 'AH's in place of the text, so that each player becomes familiar with engaging their voices at the particular points in the game in which they speak. This useful technique, used in the previous game, bridges the gap between silent play and speaking the words so that they can keep the focus on the physical demands of falling and catching. Additionally it encourages the children to express each moment of celebration and pleasure with their voices before concentrating on language and remembering the names of the clowns.

Once you have repeated the game several times and each child has played both faller and catcher, come back to the circle to share.

Chapter 11

Magic

We are such stuff
As dreams are made on. And our little life
Is rounded with a sleep

(The Tempest, IV, i, 173–5)*

Ariel torments Caliban and the clowns leading them on a journey through briars, furzes, gorse and thorns toward Prospero's cave. Prospero forgives his would-be attackers and sets Ariel free.

These final games introduce 'Shadow boxing', challenging the children's physicality and the developing the concept of playing a part. These last games focus on heightening the children's sensory awareness, stretching their imaginative skills and introducing the notion of forgiveness.

The games

- Shadow boxing
- Follow my sound
- Charming their ears
- Sounds and charms
- I miss you so
- Changing faces

The characters

- Caliban
- Stephano
- Trinculo
- Ariel
- Prospero

The targets

- Sensory awareness
- Spatial awareness
- Playing a part
- Imaginative play
- Trust and responsibility

Shadow boxing

The two clowns and Caliban are energized at the thought of killing Prospero; it represents liberty for Caliban and power for Stephano although there is doubt in the mind of Trinculo. Ariel is invisible and throws her voice pretending to be Trinculo, causing the clowns to argue.

The game introduces the physical skill of shadow boxing – throwing and receiving shadow punches – engaging the whole body with the demanding task of non-contact boxing. The technique develops the children's ability to read each other's bodies, experiencing full physical engagement but making no physical contact with each other.

The players always maintain a good safe distance between each other, enough room to 'throw a punch' without making contact with your partner.

Demonstration/playing with the children

Before playing memorize this line

My master is a tyrant

To begin, make a 'Shadow boxing' demonstration. Everyone is on their feet around the whole circle. One actor plays Caliban, staying where he is in the circle so that the whole group can see him. He begins to shadow box, assuming a boxing stance, his body alert, flexible and in constant motion. He shifts from side to side, elbows bent, arms loose and throwing punches as if he is practising on his own, alternating between throwing punches and ducking blows. After about ten seconds of demonstration and explanation he encourages the children to begin to join him and everyone begins to shadow box on the spot, throwing punches and ducking blows in their places around the circle.

Continuing to shadow box, Caliban speaks:

My master is a tyrant

He emphasizes the rhythm of the words with his boxing moves.

All the while he encourages the group to maintain their boxing. He repeats the line a few more times and with the group still boxing, he encourages everybody to speak and repeat the line:

My master is a tyrant

so that the whole group is shadow boxing and speaking Caliban's words at the same time.

Caliban and the group repeat the line a few times and then take some breathing space.

Now Caliban comes into the middle of the circle. He and the whole group resume the shadow boxing. Staying in the middle he makes eye contact with an actor around the circle and 'throws' him a punch. There is a good safe distance between them. The actor 'receives', physically responding as if he has taken a blow. Now Caliban 'throws' punches to actors and children around the circle, each receiver physically responding. When the children have grasped the idea of the game Caliban adds in the words every time he throws a punch.

Invite the children one by one to become Caliban in the middle of the circle allowing them to practise their shadow boxing and empowering them with the initiative of the game. If a child needs help, come into the circle with them and play as a duo.

Once the shadow boxing and Caliban's words are embedded in the minds and bodies of the group, everyone sits down to watch the demonstration.

Before playing memorize these words

ROUND ONE

Caliban:	My master is a tyrant
Ariel:	*(doing Trinculo's voice)* Thou liest
Caliban:	Thou liest thou jesting monkey
Trinculo:	Why I said nothing
Stephano:	Trinculo!

ROUND TWO

Caliban:	I'll yield him asleep
	Where you may knock a nail into his head
Ariel:	*(doing Trinculo's voice)* Thou liest, thou canst not
Caliban:	What a pied ninny's this?
	Thou scurvy patch!
Trinculo:	Why, I said Nothing!
Stephano	Trinculo!

ROUND THREE

Stephano:	Did you not say he lied?
Ariel:	*(doing Trinculo's voice)* Thou liest
Stephano	Do I so? Take thou that!
Trinculo:	Why, I said Nothing!
Caliban:	Ha, ha, ha.
Stephano	Monster I will kill this man

The whole game has three rounds. Depending on the concentration levels of the children, demonstrate each round separately, dividing into small groups to play with the children after each round, or demonstrate all three rounds at once before dividing up to play.

Four players are in the circle, standing in a line. Stephano faces Caliban, with good safe distance between them. Behind Caliban is Trinculo, with good safe distance between them and behind Trinculo is Ariel, very close – she is his invisible shadow. The players maintain these distances throughout the game, never making physical contact.

The clowns and Caliban take a boxing stance, all three players alert and moving, shifting their weight between their feet, knees bent, arms ready to protect and punch. Ariel is Trinculo's shadow, she stays behind him at all times as if playing the 'Shadow' game, copying everything he does.

When Caliban speaks to Stephano, he throws his shadow punches and Stephano 'receives' the shadow blows. The 'receiving' is as accurate as possible, Stephano physically ducking the punch in response to whatever is 'thrown' whilst keeping the distance between them.

Meanwhile Trinculo is knocked to the floor on each round.

When Ariel speaks she does not box, she hides behind Trinculo, imitating his voice.

ROUND ONE

Caliban:	*(throwing punches to Stephano)* My master is a tyrant
Ariel:	*(imitating Trinculo's voice)* Thou liest
Caliban:	*(turning round, throwing one punch to Trinculo, who falls to the floor)* Thou liest thou jesting monkey
Trinculo:	*(flat on the floor)* Why I said nothing
Stephano:	*(pointing at Trinculo, telling him off)*Trinculo!

Caliban, still boxing turns back to Stephano.

ROUND TWO

Caliban:	*(throwing punches to Stephano)* I'll yield him asleep Where you may knock a nail into his head
Ariel:	*(doing Trinculo's voice)* Thou liest, thou canst not
Caliban:	*(turning round, throwing one punch to Trinculo, who falls to the floor)* What a pied ninny's this? Thou scurvy patch!
Trinculo:	*(flat on the floor)*Why, I said nothing!
Stephano:	*(pointing at him, telling him off)* Trinculo!

Caliban moves a few steps away. Trinculo stands face to face with Stephano, they are in the boxing stance.

ROUND THREE

Stephano:	*(throwing punches to Trinculo)* Did you not say he lied?
Ariel:	*(doing Trinculo's voice)*Thou liest
Stephano:	*(throwing one punch to Trinculo. Trinculo falls to the floor)* Do I so? Take thou that!
Trinculo:	*(flat on the floor)* Why, I said nothing!
Caliban:	*(pointing at Trinculo)* Ha, ha, ha.
Stephano:	*(standing still)* Monster I will kill this man

The players take some breathing space, swap roles and play again.

Playing with the children

The 'Shadow boxing' encourages the children to read each other's bodies, whilst demanding a smooth flowing physicality, directly challenging their natural stiffness and rigidity, developing these skills from previous physical games. Play in small groups of three or four children. Practise the 'Shadow boxing' without words first. Make a small 'boxing circle' with your group, everyone boxing together, throwing punches into the middle of the space. Encourage the children to bend their knees, ensuring that the physical life of the boxing absorbs their whole being, from the feet upward. Before you add the words, split the children into pairs, each child taking it in turns to be thrower and receiver.

Once the boxing is embedded in their bodies, come back to your small boxing circle and introduce them to the text, demonstrating one line at a time for them to copy. Once some of the lines have been learnt, split the children back into pairs to practise boxing and speaking, ensuring that each child practises each role, maintaining the distance between them, experiencing the difference between throwing and receiving blows. Play slowly and comfortably so that each stage is fun and the children have the desire to learn more; if you give them too much too soon, they will understandably feel overwhelmed.

When you are ready to put the rounds together, giving one role to each child. Each part is enjoyable and specifically different from the others; Caliban is the fulcrum of the game with the biggest variety of lines to speak whilst Stephano receives the punches and becomes increasingly frustrated with Trinculo. Ariel has no boxing, she pops up from behind Trinculo, with the same words each time and Trinculo himself falls to the ground in each round saying 'Why I said nothing!'

Concentrating on one role only provides each child the opportunity to be part of a team, taking on a portion of responsibility for the success of the whole. Support the children as necessary; if they need you to play their part with them as a duo, ensure that you share the enjoyment, whatever the role demands. You may find yourself prompting all four parts, moving between the different children as and when they need, which can be an exhilarating experience for one and all.

When you have put a sequence together, no matter how small, come back to the circle to share. You may want to encourage the children to introduce themselves in their roles before playing.

Follow my sound

> Be not afeard; the isle is full of noises,
> Sounds and sweet airs, that give delight and hurt not.
> Sometimes a thousand twangling instruments
> Will hum about mine ears, and sometime voices
> That, if I then had waked after long sleep,
> Will make me sleep again: and then, in dreaming,
> The clouds methought would open and show riches
> Ready to drop upon me, that when I waked,
> I cried to dream again.
>
> (*The Tempest*, III, ii, 148–56)

This game is a version of 'Follow my voice' from Part I, exploring Caliban and the clowns' journey as Ariel leads them to Prospero's cave. The game encompasses sensory awareness, trust and responsibility. If you have not played 'Follow my voice' it is essential you read the demonstration and guidance in Part I (p. 112).

Demonstration

Two actors are in the circle. One plays Ariel and the other Caliban, who assumes his curved, low monster shape. They stand face-to-face approximately three paces away from each other. Ariel creates a sound with which to lead Caliban. It is Ariel's version of a 'sweet air' and it is short, repeatable and instantly recognizable.

She makes the sound once so that Caliban knows what to listen for and then Caliban closes his eyes. Ariel waits a few seconds and then makes the sound again. Caliban hears the sound and takes one step toward it, keeping his hands and arms by his sides when he moves and maintaining his curved monster shape. Ariel quietly moves to a different point in the circle, stands still and makes the sound again. Caliban takes another step toward it, sustaining his body shape.

The game continues in this way with Ariel moving as silently as possible around the circle while Caliban, keeping his eyes closed, intently listens for the next sound, taking one step toward it each time it comes. After a minute or two Ariel leads Caliban toward her with her sound and when he is in touching distance from her she gently blows air onto Caliban's forehead as if to wake him from the spell. They take a breathing space, swap roles and begin again.

Playing with the children

The basic guidance for playing 'Follow my voice' in Part I (p. 113) is essential reading for this game and should be used here depending on the needs of the child. Allow time and patience for the child to comprehend the game if they have never played before.

Encourage the children to make their sound as magical as possible – a sweet air, a twangling instrument or a humming voice. Ensure that the sound stretches the child's imaginative power as well as their vocal range and register, however it must be instantly recognizable, not a incomprehensible babble.

If the children comprehend the game and are able to play with ease, explore the characteristics of Ariel and Caliban while playing the game. Ariel is made of fire and air, her movements are light and high, whilst Caliban is made of water and earth, rooting him to the ground, heavy and slow. Encourage the children to take pleasure in these physical differences as they play, allowing the distinctions to affect every part of them, ensuring that the listening silences between the sounds are fully occupied by the expressive life of the two characters.

Ariel's breathing is fast and breathy, like a flickering flame of fire whilst Caliban's breathing is hard and slow as if each step toward the sound costs him in effort and breath. Ariel's footsteps are light, her feet barely touch the ground, shifting from foot to foot on her tiptoes whilst Caliban's feet are weighty and earth-bound – it should be hard for him to lift them. Ensure that you constantly re-invent this dynamic contrast between the two characters, finding fresh ways to express the differences.

When the child has played both parts and they have repeated the game several times come back to the circle to share.

Adding the clowns

The addition of the clowns creates further demands on the spatial awareness of the players and provides opportunity to experience increased facial expressiveness within the listening silences.

Demonstration

Four actors are in the circle, one is Ariel and the remaining three play Caliban, Stephano and Trinculo. Ariel is ready to lead them,

Caliban assumes his low curved monster shape and the clowns physically adopt their original characteristics, the fearful Trinculo and the disgusted Stephano. They stand at least one pace apart in a staggered line and Ariel stands opposite them about three paces away. She demonstrates her magical sound and the actors close their eyes.

To begin, Ariel makes one sound and all three take a step toward it, taking care not to bump into each other, using their hands and arms in front and around themselves to increase their spatial awareness. If they do touch one another, they adjust themselves to find a clear space. Ariel allows them to settle, establishing the listening silence and then makes her sound again. Once more Caliban and the clowns take one step toward it, adjusting themselves accordingly to be in their own space. After a minute or two Ariel leads them toward her with her sound and when they are in touching distance from her she gently blows air onto their foreheads to 'wake them up'. Alternatively she says 'Awake'.

They take a breathing space, swap roles and play again.

This version can be demonstrated at the end of the room, with the children watching from the opposite end if the circle is not big enough.

Playing with the children

This version of the game can be played as a whole group activity or depending on numbers you can play in small groups around the room, before joining for a final turn all together. Your small group should have a minimum of three children for the game to be valid: one to lead and two to follow. This game is complex and should be played and explored slowly, the children must keep their eyes closed, listen for Ariel's sound and take one step toward it whilst keeping distance from their fellow players. In addition the game provides an opportunity for the children to increase their expressiveness, intensifying their basic facial characteristic with each step they take toward the noise – Caliban becomes heavier, Trinculo more fearful and Stephano more disgusted.

When you have played in small groups, come together and play the game as a whole group activity. One child can play Ariel and the rest of the children join the actors, choosing whether to play Caliban or one of the clowns. As leader, remain open-eyed and in charge of the game, encouraging and supporting actors and children if they need and silently communicating with the child playing Ariel. The whole group position themselves at one end of the room, assuming their specific characteristics. If a child needs assistance then an actor can pair up, holding hands or physically supporting them as they move forward.

Ariel then demonstrates her sound whilst Caliban and clowns close their eyes. The room should be completely silent. Ariel begins by making her specific sound and the whole group takes one step toward it. They can use their hands and arms to feel their way forward, spreading out if they need to find more space and then they wait, attentive, listening for the next sound. Ariel waits for them to settle and for the listening silence in the room to become palpable. She then makes her sound again and the group takes another step toward her, maintaining their specific characteristics and repeating the heightened, attentive experience once more. In this way the child playing Ariel is in control of the whole group, leading them all around the room, with silent support and encouragement from the leader if necessary.

To finish the game Ariel blows air onto the foreheads of Calibans and clowns, or she simply says 'Awake' at which point everybody opens their eyes and another child can have a turn at playing Ariel. It's also possible to have two or three Ariels working as a team leading the group around the circle and taking it in turns to make the sound. The game must always be played slowly, with a short settling period before each sound for everyone to experience the listening silence. This group version of the game is complete when each child has had a turn as Ariel.

Charming their ears

> At last I left them,
> I'th filthy mantled pool beyond your cell
> Dancing up to th' chins
>
> (*The Tempest*, IV, i, 202–4)

Ariel leads the drunken and foolish Caliban and clowns on a treacherous journey toward Prospero. Narratively, this game follows directly from 'Sounds and sweet airs', offering language skills and a further exploration of imaginative play.

Demonstration

Before playing memorize these lines

> They smote the air for breathing in their faces;
> Beat the ground for kissing of their feet;
> They prick'd their ears,
> Advanced their eyelids,
> Lifted up their noses as if they smelt music

Two actors are in the circle. One plays Ariel and the other Caliban, who assumes his curved, low monster shape and a drunken face. They stand face-to-face approximately three paces away from each other. Caliban closes his eyes and keeps them closed for the whole game, he is listening for Ariel's voice whilst Ariel is watching him. Ariel is using her eyes whilst Caliban is using his ears.

Ariel speaks the first line:

> They smote the air for breathing in their faces;

Caliban embodies this description, beating at the air in front of his face.

When he is finished Ariel waits for him to settle and then speaks the next line:

> They beat the ground for kissing of their feet;

Caliban embodies this description, stamping on the ground below him.

When he is finished Ariel waits for him to settle and then speaks the next line:

> They prick'd their ears,

Caliban embodies this description, alerting his ears like an animal, his whole attention focused on his ears.

When he is finished Ariel waits for him to settle and then speaks the next line:

> Advanced their eyelids,

Caliban embodies this description, focusing his whole attention on moving his eyelids forward.

When he is finished Ariel waits for him to settle and then speaks the next line:

And lifted up their noses as if they smelt music.

Caliban embodies this description focusing his whole attention on his nose, moving it as though it could 'hear'.

Caliban finishes and opens his eyes.

The players take a breathing space, swap roles and play again.

Playing with the children

Begin to explore the game with the children by letting them explore the role of Caliban, suggesting they keep their eyes open, and ensuring that they completely understand the words and the actions. Demonstrate your version of Caliban, showing them how to bring the game to life, rather than telling them. If they are struggling you can break the game down to five instructional verbs for initial clarity.

Smite the air, **beat** the ground, **prick** the ears, **advance** the eyelids and **lift** the nose.

Isolating the verbs and allowing the children to give them full attention is at the heart of the game. Encourage the children to focus entirely on each specific command, taking as long as they need to explore and embody the physical life inherent to the verb.

There is a distinct difference between the two roles, Ariel's role is language-based whilst Caliban's is sensory. Ariel has the power of the game, leading Caliban through the series of actions whilst Caliban's role is entirely receptive, embodying and experiencing each of the five commands. Ensure that the children swap roles to experience both sides of the game. After they have played with eyes open, encourage the child to play Caliban with eyes closed, heightening their sensory awareness and developing their levels of trust.

Before adding the clowns, explore two different ways to approach the game. The first, as described, is to isolate each action and explore them separately, each one replacing the one before. The second version is to embody each stage in addition to the previous ones, so that there is no settling time between them and the end of the game actively engages Caliban in all five 'states'.

When you are ready, come back to the circle to share.

Adding the clowns

Demonstration

Four actors are in the circle, playing Ariel, Caliban, Stephano and Trinculo. The two clowns join Caliban, taking a position one pace away from each other and assuming their starting expressions – Caliban is low and curved, Stephano is disgusted and Trinculo is fearful; all three adopt an additional expression of drunken foolishness. They close their eyes and listen for Ariel's voice. Ariel stands facing them, a few paces away. Caliban and the clowns will use their ears and Ariel will use her eyes.

Ariel speaks the first line:

> They smote the air for breathing in their faces;

Caliban and the clowns embody this description, beating at the air in front of their faces.

When they are finished Ariel waits for them to settle and then speaks the next line:

> They beat the ground for kissing of their feet;

Caliban and the clowns embody this description, stamping on the ground below them.

When they are finished Ariel waits for them to settle and then speaks the next line:

> They prick'd their ears,

Caliban and the clowns embody this description, alerting their ears like animals, their whole attention focused on their ears.

When they are finished Ariel waits for them to settle and then speaks the next line:

> Advanced their eyelids,

Caliban and the clowns embody this description, focusing their whole attention on moving their eyelids forward.

When they are finished Ariel waits for them to settle and then speaks the next line:

> And lifted up their noses as if they smelt music.

Caliban and the clowns embody this description focusing their whole attention on their noses.

When they have finished they open their eyes.

The players take a breathing space, swap roles and play again.

Playing with the children

Play in small groups, adjusting your approach according to the needs of the children. Begin to explore the game by letting them play Caliban, Stephano or Trinculo. Allow the children to choose which one they would like to play, encouraging them to embrace the distinct characteristics of each one, adding the quality of drunkenness for an extra challenge.

Play the game working through the four stages of playing: eyes open followed by eyes closed, and exploring the verbs separately followed by exploring them together. It's important that each child gets to play Ariel and also plays at least one of the 'followers', in the interest of time they do not have to play all three. When they have played both leader and follower at least once, come back to the circle to share.

Sounds and charms

Caliban and the clowns are led through the island by the sound of Ariel, responding to her magic as established in 'Follow my sound'. This game is a combination of the previous two, wherein Ariel blends her tasks together, leading Caliban and the clowns around the room with her sound whilst instructing them with their responses. The game is complex, challenging the children's sensory and spatial awareness, providing the opportunity for them to take initiative within the game and heighten their powers of concentration.

Demonstration

Two actors are in the circle. One plays Ariel and the other Caliban, who assumes his curved, low monster shape. They stand face-to-face about three paces away from each other. Ariel creates her sound with which to lead Caliban. It is her version of a 'sweet air', short, repeatable and instantly recognizable.

She makes the sound once so that Caliban knows what to listen for and then Caliban closes his eyes. Ariel waits a few seconds and then makes the sound. Caliban takes one step toward it.

Ariel now speaks the first line:

They smote the air for breathing in their faces;

Caliban embodies this description, beating at the air in front of his face.

Ariel quietly moves to a different point in the circle, stands still and waits for Caliban to settle. She makes the sound again. Caliban takes another step toward it, sustaining his body shape.

After a few seconds, Ariel speaks the next line:

They beat the ground for kissing of their feet;

Caliban embodies this description, stamping on the ground below him.

Ariel quietly moves to a different point in the circle, stands still and waits for Caliban to settle. She makes the sound again. Caliban takes another step toward it, sustaining his body shape.

After a few seconds, Ariel speaks the next line:

They prick'd their ears,

Caliban embodies this description, alerting his ears like an animal, his whole attention focused on his ears.

Ariel quietly moves to a different point in the circle, stands still and waits for Caliban to settle. She makes the sound again. Caliban takes another step toward it, sustaining his body shape.

After a few seconds, Ariel speaks the next line:

Advanced their eyelids,

Caliban embodies this description, focusing his whole attention on moving his eyelids forward.

Ariel quietly moves to a different point in the circle, stands still and waits for Caliban to settle. She makes the sound again. Caliban takes another step toward it, sustaining his body shape.

After a few seconds, Ariel speaks the last line:

> And lifted up their noses as if they smelt music.

Caliban embodies this description focusing his whole attention on his nose.

By this time Ariel is within touching distance of Caliban and gently blows air onto Caliban's forehead as if to wake him from the spell. They take a breathing space, swap roles and begin again.

Playing with the children

Ensure that you have played both previous games before you try this one. Begin by letting the children play Caliban, encouraging them to close their eyes, ensuring them that they can trust you. If the child is fearful set a boundary for the game: agree to begin with your instruction 'Close your eyes' finishing with 'Open your eyes' and that whilst their eyes are closed you will only give one sound followed by one instruction for them to follow. They can then open their eyes. If they are happy to play in this way, slowly build the number of sounds and instructions you give as they become more confident. If you do set boundaries or make agreements ensure that you stick to them even if you are tempted to push the children further within the moments of playing. They should never feel as though they have been tricked into doing something even if that something was an improvement; allow the children to have ownership of their progress.

Encourage children who are comfortable closing their eyes to fully tackle the challenges offered in the game. The 'blindness' provides an opportunity for them to expand their own limits of trust, the more they play the game the greater their sense of trust will become. Their levels of concentration will also be challenged, the alternation between sound and instruction demands increased attentiveness. Finally their sense of imaginative play will be enhanced, as the game offers an opportunity for the child to interpret Caliban's journey through the embodiment of Ariel's instructions.

When you have repeated the game a few times come back to the circle to share.

Adding the clowns

The addition of the clowns increases the challenges of spatial awareness between the players.

Demonstration

Four actors are in the circle, playing Ariel, Caliban, Stephano and Trinculo. The two clowns join Caliban, taking a position one pace away from each other and assuming their starting expressions – Caliban is low and curved, Stephano is disgusted and Trinculo is fearful; all three adopt an additional expression of drunken foolishness. They close their eyes and listen for Ariel's voice. Ariel stands facing them, a few paces away. Caliban and the clowns will use their ears and Ariel will use her eyes. She creates her sound with which to lead Caliban and the clowns. It is her version of a 'sweet air', short, repeatable and instantly recognizable.

She makes the sound once so that they know what to listen for and then they close their eyes. Ariel waits a few seconds and then makes the sound. Caliban and the clowns take one step toward it.

Ariel now speaks the first line:

They smote the air for breathing in their faces;

From here they play the game exactly as before, alternating between sound and instruction, taking extra care of the spatial awareness between the players.

Playing with the children

The addition of the clowns provides one last test of spatial awareness between the three players being led. Ensure that they begin an arm's length away from each other and play two versions of the game. The first allows them to use their arms and hands to guide themselves in their 'blind step' toward Ariel, if they bump into each other they can immediately adjust their position.

In the second version they keep their arms and hands by their sides for the 'blind step', bringing an increased sense of cautionary tension into the game, further heightening the children's sensory awareness. When the children open their eyes at the end of this version, they are often surprised to see their physical relationship to the other players.

When the children have played leader and one of the followers, come back to the circle to share.

I miss you so

At the very end of the play Prospero grants Ariel her liberty.

This game represents their moment of farewell; it involves eye contact, the heartbeat rhythm and a high level of physical trust between the players. The heartbeat rhythm creates a comfortable environment within which the children feel safe at the beginning of each session, providing the background for their initial exploration of facial expressiveness. This game builds on that trust introducing a purposeful break in the heartbeat rhythm, representing the flight of Ariel. The 'missed heartbeat' offers a rush of adrenalin and excitement concurrent with Ariel's flight.

Demonstration

Before playing memorize these lines

Ariel: I go, I go
Prospero: I'll miss you so
Ariel/Prospero: So, so, so.

Two players are in the circle, playing Prospero and Ariel. To begin they stand facing each other very close, their toes almost touching one another. Prospero crosses his hands out in front of him, offering them to Ariel. She takes hold of his hands or wrists whichever is more comfortable. Their arms are crossed. They slowly lean backwards bending their knees and keeping their feet stationary, sharing each other's weight. They maintain eye contact during the whole game.

When they have leant back as far as they can they let go of their right hands and place them on their hearts. They begin to beat out the rhythm of the heartbeat. They are supporting each other with their left hands or wrists, left elbow slightly bent and flexible, they share each other's weight, knees bent, leaning back as far as possible.

They create a strong steady heartbeat rhythm between them and after a few seconds they begin to speak. Their words fit perfectly with their rhythm.

Ariel:	I go, I go
Prospero:	I'll miss you so
Ariel:	So
Prospero:	So
Ariel/Prospero:	(together) So

Immediately after the last 'So' both players take a deep breath and make a full sweeping 'backstroke' circle with their right arms. The movement is releasing and powerful, representing Ariel's moment of liberty.

Described in slow motion the full movement is thus: breathing in, sweep your right arm up and over your head in an arc, down past your thigh and back to the starting point where, breathing out, you swap hands with your partner. To swap, you simultaneously let go of each other's left hand or wrist as you grasp your partner's right hand or wrist creating a hiatus of physical excitement between you as if you have 'missed a heartbeat'. This provides the POE.

Both players are now supporting each other with their right hands and immediately place their left hands on their hearts re-establishing the heartbeat rhythm. They settle back down into the leaning back position, knees and elbows supportive and flexible.

After a few seconds they begin to speak again, repeating the sequence three more times. On the final turn they omit the sweep and this time pull each other up to standing, coming close together to speak the final unison 'So'.

Each 'missed heartbeat' creates a mini POE.

Take a breathing space and swap roles to play again. In swapping roles, the only difference is the words that are spoken, the physical experience is the same for both players.

Playing with the children

The game can be difficult for the children on many levels, but has the distinct advantage of being played almost as if the partners were mirror images of each other, providing the opportunity to teach the game through copying. If the child is very anxious about the leaning back aspect of the game, you can create a simpler version. Sit up on your knees, facing the child about an arm's length away and encourage them to mirror you. Place the palms of your hands up in front of you and place the child's palms against yours. Push against their palms with a little pressure, encouraging them to push against yours, creating some traction between you. If the child comes back with absolutely nothing, gently hold hands with them, interlocking fingers, pushing and pulling forward and backward, to introduce the idea of the pressure. Offer the child palpable encouragement if they start to push against your hands.

When you have established a good physical relationship, begin to speak the words, prompting the child if needs be. To circle the arms, take a breath in, lift your hands above your heads, keeping the child's hands pressed to yours (or holding their hands and guiding them) and make a sweeping semi-circle down to the floor. Then on your breath out, let go of each other's hands and quickly bring them back to the palm to palm starting point, creating the 'missed heartbeat'. The physical hand-to-heart activity is omitted from this version, therefore ensure that you speak the words with a strong sense of the heartbeat rhythm, which is embedded within the language, guaranteeing the game's connection to the pulse.

Encourage all the children, no matter which version of the game they are able to achieve to embrace the moment of the 'missed heartbeat', bringing the excitement of Ariel's freedom to life. Ensure that the breathing is concurrent with the action each time, the breath in synchronized with the upward sweep of the arms and the breath out representing the missed heartbeat and the thrill of liberty.

When you have repeated the game a few times come back to the circle to share.

Changing faces

This thing of darkness I
Acknowledge mine

(*The Tempest*, V, i, 330–1)

At the end of the play Prospero and Caliban appear to reach an accord and although there remains a degree of ambiguity around their relationship, both characters seem to express self-knowledge, shame and forgiveness.

This last game is a version of 'Waking up' from *A Midsummer Night's Dream*. The game uses a combination of the heartbeat rhythm, eye contact and the sense of touch for the children to experience an expressive transformation from anger to peace.

Demonstration

Before playing memorize these lines

Ariel: If you beheld him
              Your affections would become tender
Prospero/Caliban: Dost thou think so spirit?
Ariel: Mine would Sir, were I human
Prospero/Caliban: And mine shall

Three actors are in the circle, they play Prospero, Caliban and Ariel. Prospero and Caliban sit back-to-back on the floor in the middle of the circle. They assume angry faces and place their hands on their hearts as if they cannot bear to look at one another. Ariel stands a few paces away from them, she assumes a worried face and places her hand on her heart.

To begin all three players start to make their heartbeats, Prospero and Caliban make a strong, slow and angry rhythm whilst Ariel's rhythm is twice as fast, as if her heart is racing with panic. She begins to move quickly around the pair watching them. Prospero and Caliban stare into the distance. All three players maintain their specific heartbeat rhythms throughout this first stage.

After a few seconds Ariel speaks to Prospero and Caliban:

If you beheld him
Your affections would become tender

They hear her but make an angry grumble, trying to ignore her and continuing with their angry heartbeats.

Ariel continues to circle them. She repeats the line:

If you beheld him
Your affections would become tender

Again, they hear her but make an even angrier grumble, trying to ignore her and continuing with their angry heartbeats.

Ariel continues to circle them. Finally she speaks again, emphasizing the final word:

If you beheld him
Your affections would become tender

This time Prospero and Caliban turn their heads to look at Ariel. They drop their hands. Ariel continues to beat out her speedy heartbeat rhythm.

Prospero and Caliban speak:

Dost thou think so spirit?

Ariel speaks:

Mine would Sir, were I human

As she says 'human', she changes the rhythm of her heartbeat from speedy to steady as if adopting a 'tender human' rhythm. This is the only sound to be heard, it continues until the end of the game.

Prospero and Caliban slowly begin to turn their bodies around toward each other, allowing their anger to melt away. When they are facing each other they slowly lift their faces up so that they begin to find each other's eyes. When they make eye contact, they hold it for as long as possible and begin to smile. Finally they raise their hands up to make contact palm-to-palm. They speak:

And mine shall.

After some breathing space the actors swap roles and demonstrate again.

Playing with the children

The heart of the game is toward the end, when the characters' facial expressions change from angry to peaceful in response to the idea of forgiveness. If the children are struggling with the words play a simpler silent version. Two players simply sit back-to-back making angry faces and heartbeats. They slowly turn round to face each other and change their faces and heartbeats to express peacefulness.

It is quite hard not to laugh during the end of the game as the tension melts away and eye contact is made and this is to be encouraged. It should be fun. Encourage the child to enjoy the full eye contact and palm-to-palm moment as if it is a reward for all their hard work.

Encourage children at the higher end of the spectrum to explore the 'spirit' quality of Ariel, ensuring that they experience the transformation from her speedy panicked heartbeat to her slower tender human heartbeat. You can add in the elements of fire and air to her body shape and voice if the children have the cognition. If they are playing Prospero or Caliban ensure that the experience at the beginning of the game – no eye contact, angry faces and thumping heartbeat is in opposition to the sensations at the end of the game – full eye contact, peaceful smiles and palm to each other's palm.

When the children have repeated the game and swapped the roles come back to the circle to share.

Chapter 12

A resource for playing with the children

I have compiled this list through consultation with the actors of the research project in Ohio who have played the games almost every week for the last two years. Some of the tips are direct quotes from the book and some are direct quotes from the actors. All are chosen as quick, key reminders of how to play with the children, giving you confidence in what can sometimes feel like an impossible task.

- To be present in the moment is one of the all time best notes for an actor and essential when playing these games with children.
- Your ultimate aim no matter where the children are on the spectrum is for them to experience what a game <u>feels</u> like.
- Learn the child's name as soon as you meet them and always use it.
- Use concise language to instruct the children. Choose a few words rather than long sentences.
- Never give up on the child's ability to play.
- The opening games of 'Heartbeat hellos' and 'Throwing the face' are as essential for the actors as they are for the children.
- Shakespeare's plays are packed with moments of transcendence and these are embodied within the games as 'Points of Ecstasy', moments where effort culminates in achievement and it's clear that the game has been accomplished. The expression POE is found throughout the book and serves as a reminder that the games must be pleasurable; the children's communicative progress is dependent on sharing a sense of playfulness with the adult.
- Your role as prompter is key, you are offering the child the stimulus to speak.

- Connect yourself to the child's time frame rather than expecting them to meet yours. *'Take your time'* is a phrase worth repeating more than almost any other: a beautiful, powerful phrase. Allow the children to feel that you know they understand you and that you understand they are doing their best to achieve the physical task.
- Take your time especially with children who struggle with cognition, and adapt each game to suit their needs. Every time the child makes a physical transformation, no matter how much support they have received from you in order to make it, is another step toward their communicative progress.
- Ensure that you are working with the child at their own pace and not missing out any of the necessary steps in order to get a final result; playing each phase of the game itself is result enough.
- The trying *is* the intervention.
- The trance games directly challenge the physical 'stiffness' often associated with autism inviting a flow of movement from one person to the next as well as challenging the children's spatial awareness and encouraging longer periods of concentrated eye focus.
- It's important that the children feel they are sharing the games with you and that you are truly enjoying yourself. The beneficial side of the work is embedded deep in the games and begins to take root through a shared pleasurable experience between actor and child.
- Make physical contact with the children with confidence.
- Playing the games should feel as if time stops and that the child has a boundless opportunity to explore and embody sensations and feeling, which may otherwise be overlooked.
- The children's communicative progress is on-going and long term, continuing for months and years. The balance between pushing them to achieve communicative breakthroughs and allowing them to feel safe is always in flux. Keep your priority on building their trust and sense of safety, without that they will never make any self-discoveries. As the drama sessions become part of their weekly life they usually find the games easier to play even though the games themselves may become more complex – this has proved true with every group of children I have worked with.

Photo 28 Catching the face (photo © Melissa Lee)

Photo 29 Throwing the face (photo © Melissa Lee)

- At the heart of the work you are pinpointing what the child can't do, and doing it with them until they can.
- If the child has issues with time introduce a large clock and allow exactly two minutes for the duration of a game. It works wonders for any game.
- The child's potential for personal change is contained within the humour and playfulness with which you demonstrate and share the game.
- Use the introduction method from *'Playing a part'* (p. 73) to introduce any character and any game.
- Your fundamental aim is to use Shakespeare as a means of waking the children up to their own lives; the plays ask more questions than they give answers and at best the work empowers the children to do the same, taking enquiring steps into unknown personal territory which they would otherwise not have the opportunity to do.
- It's useful to think of the act of 'playing' as 'changing': to play is to change.
- When demonstrating and playing with the children experiment with turning the volume of your voice down in relation to your emotions and encourage the children to do the same – the more intense the emotion the quieter your voice.
- 'Failure' is opportunity. New games only emerge because something doesn't work and you have the curiosity to try another strategy.
- The games are constantly evolving, they belong to the children who play them.
- Do ensure that an enthusiastic suggestion from a child is greeted with equal enthusiasm from yourself and that you always try out their ideas. These games would not exist in their current form if that had not been the case.

Instructive playfulness

When playing with the children you must be 100 per cent committed to acting your part whether you are the lovestruck Titania, Caliban the monster or any of the characters throughout the book. At the same time stay alive to the fact that the child may need your help. Stay ready – whilst playing – to give instruction and lead the children toward their communicative progress. Your aim is to help the child overcome their difficulties whilst you continue playing and acting, gently instructing them if they need prompting with the line or help with any number of issues, physical and expressive, at any one time. With this in place the experience of playing with the children remains absorbing and creative for both of you. This technique is at the heart of the work; without it the games may seem impossible.

Afterword

There's no success like failure
And failure's no success at all

(Bob Dylan, 'Love minus zero')

A few years ago I was giving workshops at a Shakespeare conference in the north of England playing with groups of local children for an audience of academics, educationalists and fans of Shakespeare. One such fan, a middle-aged Welsh gentleman of great enthusiasm bounded up to me at the end of a session and embraced me. 'You've reminded me to play' he said with his sing-song accent 'You've reminded me why I love Shakespeare, after all he didn't write *serious's* ...he wrote *plays*'. It was meant as a compliment and I took it as such, although I am serious about these games, not serious about myself but serious about playing. The more seriously I take the art of playing with children the more fun it reveals itself to be.

I'm an actress. I have been acting for well over thirty years in a roller-coaster of a career, the twists and turns of which have undoubtedly informed my journey in creating these games for children. I've played major roles at the Royal Shakespeare Company in Stratford, London and New York, toured the world with the Icelandic theatre company Vesturport and played the leading role in the National Theatre's most infamous failure under the stewardship of Sir Peter Hall when I was just nineteen. In 2002 whilst still very much in the middle of my acting life, I began to create games for children and set up Touchstone Shakespeare Theatre in order to introduce Shakespeare to children with no access to the arts.

At the heart of my endeavour was a self-imposed investigation into Shakespeare's validity today. To understand how I arrived at this point may offer a deeper understanding of the value I place upon 'being in the moment' and the power of playfulness. To start with I lay no claim to formal education or training. Not having had the opportunity for a literate education but having the interest and instinct for one has led me to a lifetime of self-schooling. In my late teens I worked my way through Dickens and Dostoevsky whereas my peers, at drama school or university and envious of my 'success' found the very same books a chore. Being completely self-taught I'm curious about ways of learning that appear to be outside the general consensus. With hindsight I see that these autodidactic tendencies have unconsciously informed my ways of working with children and young people, allowing me a freedom to experiment unconstrained by orthodox procedure.

My first job was playing 'The Mistress' in *Evita* taking over in the original production in London's West End. I was seventeen, sitting on a suitcase every night singing four minutes of song and not feeling as if I particularly belonged anywhere. I have a distinct memory of standing in the wings of the Prince Edward Theatre watching the dancers do their slow motion tango toward the end of each performance. I loved how time seemed to stand still in a secret ritual I would half close my eyes so that the dancers became a blurred shape of red and black lit by dazzling light moving through time and space to the music. I would allow myself to wonder how and why anybody was alive.

Two years later and utterly inexperienced in the ways of the world, I landed the leading role in a musical at the National Theatre. *Jean Seberg* was a biographical piece about the tragic life of the eponymous heroine, it was directed by Sir Peter Hall with music by Marvin Hamlisch. There was huge anticipation about this show and indeed a big fuss about me before we opened. I had a very high-powered agent who had seen me in the workshop performance and pronouncing that a star was born had signed me up that day. A Broadway contract sat on his desk ready for me to sign once the show opened in London, so certain were the creative team of success.

Their predictions were akin to the unsinkable claims for the *Titanic*. The show was a disaster; the press night was continually postponed, as I had to perform in a wheelchair due to a twisted ankle. Another actor fell from a twenty-foot high platform and through his injuries had to be replaced. The production resulted in two nervous breakdowns within the creative team and once it had finally opened – to savage reviews – it was given notice before we'd finished the allotted forty performances. *Jean Seberg* sank without trace and needless to say that Broadway contract got shelved to garner nothing but dust and all interest in me dissolved like dew.

I was twenty years old and at the epicentre of inflated egos, broken dreams and theatrical hyperbole. Overnight I acquired heightened radar for insincerity and developed a self-deprecating sense of humour. I couldn't stomach the superficiality so often endemic within my profession and wanted only to be engaged in brave, honest, artistic endeavours in rooms with like-minded people. I had a fearless attitude toward work, which culminated in Paris at the Theatre Mogador a few years later playing Sally Bowles in French directed by Jérôme Savary. This was theatre at its most pleasurable, romantic and fun. The show had an ever-changing rota of circus performers plus 'ladies of the night' from Pigalle whom Savary would invite to sit and smoke on stage; he claimed they added character to the evening and told me to be as charismatic as them. The production played to packed audiences of a thousand people every night and in truth everything I have performed in since has been tame in comparison.

After living in Paris I stopped working in the theatre, volunteering at the Terrence Higgins Trust in London after the death of a close friend from AIDS in 1987. I organized an enormous fundraising campaign – Shop Assistance – placing famous people in the shops, bars and restaurants of Covent Garden for a day, for which the businesses donated their profits to the trust. It was a one-off event, raising money and awareness by the bucket-load and something I remain proud of to this day. Had I put the same amount of energy into my own career this story may have been very different. During this time I worked with Frontliners – a self-help group of men and women diagnosed with HIV – all of whom were facing their own mortalities whilst dealing with the huge prejudices that came with the disease in those days. I have never met a more generous group of people in my life, their gallows humour was a privilege to share as they campaigned for themselves and others in the face of their misfortune. In the space of a year I attended fifteen funerals.

Success crept up on me in the shape of 'Lola' in *The Blue Angel*, directed by Trevor Nunn for the RSC. I wasn't originally cast in the role – Trevor's first choice had left rehearsals and I was brought in at the last minute with barely any time before the scheduled opening. Having been around the world of cabaret artists and 'charismatic ladies of the night' in Paris I knew exactly how to perform this piece.

We opened in Stratford at the brand-new refurbished Other Place Theatre after only ten days of rehearsal. The show was a smash hit, creating for me a surreal experience having lived through the smash failure at the National ten years before.

The Blue Angel doubled with a production of *Measure for Measure*, using the same cast and set. Before arriving in London's West End the two productions made a lengthy small-scale tour around the UK. There was actually not much about the tour that was small – five pantechnicon lorries would roll into a town and set up in a tiny school or leisure centre at least twenty miles away from the nearest big city. Most evenings the locals from the town would walk right past our posters to go to play darts in the pub. Meanwhile an enthusiastic theatre-going audience, well-versed in Shakespeare and theatre would make the twenty-mile sojourn from the big cities – Newcastle, Bristol or Glasgow – to see the RSC.

It was abundantly clear to me that just because the company turned up on people's doorsteps with RSC productions it didn't guarantee a flicker of interest from a local non-theatre going audience. And it was expensive. This was in the days before RSC outreach and education had grown into the department it is nowadays, directly tackling these issues. The sight of men choosing to go to the pub rather than see our shows infuriated me and sowed the seeds for the work I was to begin ten years later – taking Shakespeare to people with no access to the arts. It was during this same tour that I worked at the men's prison in Darlington inventing the non-scripted Shakespeare workshop, which I talk about in the introduction of the book.

Having scored a big success with *The Blue Angel* offers for more leading roles poured in whilst privately the experience of singing and dancing and being in musicals bore no representation to my inner life. I thought long and hard about my experience in the prison where I had felt so completely in my element but I had no idea at the time how to replicate that work. Outwardly I slowly began to change the course of my life and I never did another musical again. Two years later I played 'Rosalind' for the English Touring Theatre, my first major Shakespearean role. On the advice of a friend I visited the Shakespeare Centre Library in Stratford-upon-Avon a few weeks before rehearsals, sat down with a copy of the first folio and turned to *As You Like It*. I'd never seen the folio before. I read the play from beginning to end almost without breathing and several times it made me cry. The beauty of the language was not just in its sound and rhythm but also in its very appearance on the page, unfettered and achingly old. I sat in the library in the sunlight on a July afternoon and I could have stayed forever.

I went on to play 'Rosalind' and I won a TMA best actress award for my performance. I dedicated it to Graham Taylor the ex-England football manager, who had that week been sacked from Wolverhampton Wanderers. I'd met him earlier in the car park and told him what a huge fan of his I was, he'd shaken my hand and wished me luck. I bestowed my award to him, saying that I was sure he knew more about success and failure than I ever could. I should probably have thanked the director of the show, and made a more normal acceptance speech but the 'Seberg effect' of not taking myself too seriously is deeply ingrained and pops up at the most unexpected of times.

In early 2002 I was at the end of a third season with the RSC playing 'Constance' in *King John* in Stratford and at the Barbican in London. It had been very successful, but I increasingly found myself in conflict with those in authority. I was pestered by a voice in my head telling me that I hadn't even begun to explore my own creative potential – the memory of my workshop in the Darlington prison continued to bang against my skull. I was preoccupied with the notion that Shakespeare's plays have untapped powers, inaccessible to many people through traditional means of performance and I was deeply frustrated by the overused maxim that 'Shakespeare is for everyone'. I absolutely agreed in the universality of Shakespeare's plays but I knew that the men in Darlington prison would not have been empowered by *Measure for Measure* back in 1991 had I not found a means of unlocking the language for them and giving them the tools to own it for themselves. For me it sounded lazy to just say Shakespeare belonged to the people – I wanted to test that out.

I don't claim originality in what I was thinking, there are artists all over the world taking drama to those who wouldn't normally see it but I wanted to do it myself. In the summer of 2002 I was absorbed with the idea of inventing ways to unlock Shakespeare in a non-theatrical context. I didn't want to become a disgruntled bystander – thinking I knew better than others but never doing anything about it – so I set up my own company.

I created Touchstone Shakespeare Theatre enlisting the help of four younger actors, setting it up as a charity dedicated to offer Shakespeare to children and young people who have no access to the arts. With no track record we gave free workshops at the primary school my own children were attending and used the opportunity to create and establish a first set of games. These were based around *A Midsummer Night's Dream* and developed into the games for children with autism in this book. I had so many ideas and so much unbridled enthusiasm that the company snowballed very quickly. I was creating workshops and testing them out on children, sleeplessly absorbed in how to bring Shakespeare alive whilst at the same time fundraising and endlessly offering myself and my company to the places I wanted to be – special schools and prisons.

The Glebe project at the Glebe special school in Bromley came about through chance, the result of my search for somewhere to work and a teacher's search for someone to provide 'much needed drama in a special school'. We were given three years' worth of money from a charitable foundation and it was here that we began working with children with autism. I was in effect handed an opportunity to experiment and create my own way of playing with children, without which this work would never have developed.

We worked at the Glebe once a week, giving workshops to different groups of children defined by their particular needs. We created specific games of Shakespeare for each group, using different plays and applying various drama techniques. The school was a turbulent environment, accommodating a large number of confused and troubled children. In the midst of this chaotic setting was one designated class for children with autism called The Unit. As the project got underway, it was with this core group of 14 autistic children, aged between 12–15 years old that the games took on a whole new meaning.

It became clear that at the core of every game there was something that these children found impossible. It was as if I had distilled Shakespeare's exploration of human communication to its essence and then offered it to children for whom these exact communicative qualities were either very difficult or seemingly impracticable. Through playing the games they discovered for themselves that what had seemed impossible was in fact potentially attainable. As we got to know the children we created specific games to challenge their unique difficulties, thereby building a body of work designed to combat the complex demands of autism. This original group of children effectively taught me how to teach them and the games could never have evolved without them.

I built up a strong repertoire of work with Touchstone working with at-risk teenagers and children with autism in schools across the UK. I continued to teach at St Mary's and St Peter's primary school (the first school we had gone to), working on *A Midsummer Night's Dream*, *The Tempest*, *King Lear*, *Twelfth Night* and *Macbeth* with 4–11 year olds. I also created *The Beckton Lear* – a production of *King Lear* performed by at-risk teenagers in Beckton, London. After working for four years I was burnt out with only myself to blame, delegation had not been one of my strong points and I had overwhelmed myself with administration. I resigned and almost immediately began working with Vesturport, the Icelandic theatre company in a new production of *Metamorphosis* – a show that has taken me around the world. Performing with these Icelandic actors is the nearest I have come to working for Jérôme Savary in Paris; they are brave, humorous and completely present on stage. With them I feel totally at home.

In 2009 I returned to the RSC to play 'Hermione' in *The Winter's Tale* and 'Goneril' in *King Lear* and as part of my contract I was to work with the Education department giving workshops for children with autism at Hay Lane School in Colindale, London. At the time I had no idea that these workshops would lead to the research project at OSU and indeed this book. I was to be giving workshops by day and performing at night. On my first day at Hay Lane I found myself in a classroom with seven children. Not one of them could speak. Not one of them had English as a first language at home. It seemed that not one of them was going to sit still for more than ten seconds and they'd already ripped up the circle of masking tape I'd laid out on the floor. It was nine o'clock in the morning,

A couple of teaching assistants who'd been told they had to 'watch the children do drama' were eyeing me with suspicion, making no attempt to help. Gone were my team of actors and gone indeed were the Glebe children I'd known so well. I managed to settle the room down for a few minutes and I made some heartbeats; my voice sounded very lonely on its own, a far cry from the nurturing womblike wall of sound my team and I used to make. I'll never forget the look of contempt from the teaching assistants when I suggested they could 'catch Bottom's donkey face'. It was an inauspicious beginning.

I'd organized myself in exactly the same way I had at the Glebe. I was to work there one day a week, giving five sessions with different groups defined by their specific needs, but here the similarity ended. These groups would include children with no verbal skills, whose grasp of English was so limited that it would be fruitless to begin with the 'Mind's eye' dream sequence as they wouldn't understand the questions. I had been stripped of all comforts that had facilitated my work at the Glebe, namely the small band of actors who'd accompanied me and the relative cognition of the children, which had enabled us to make progress comparatively smoothly. I had bare essentials that I believed in, the power of the heartbeat to soothe and the resonance of Shakespeare's definition of love. Over the years I had developed methods of playing with children with autism, the big difference was that now I would be doing all the demonstrating and sharing alone.

Hay Lane became my experiment, as if children for whom communication was seemingly impossible were putting my games to the test. At the beginning nothing appeared to work. I would return home feeling that I had completely failed these children and that I was a fraud. I was very hard on myself; the great monoliths of Shakespeare and autism seemed to have defeated me, but I continued doggedly, carving out a whole new approach to the Heartbeat Circle for non-verbal children. The children at Hay Lane have a profound disassociation between body and mind, and once up on their feet they need to have their bodies moved for them in order to learn how to play even the simplest of games. There were a handful of inspiring teachers at the school without whom I would have been lost. From them I learnt very specifically that forging a robust physical relationship with the child was essential in order for them to have any chance of playing. I began to teach with more confidence.

And after about six months I began to realize that my teaching had changed beyond recognition. These children were teaching me about reading people, trying to understand what others are thinking and feeling that they can't articulate for themselves. I think the games at the Glebe had always been doing that but it wasn't until I adapted them for these harder to reach children that I began to understand it. Second, I began to understand the power and beauty of teaching with patience. At the Glebe patience had meant that we allowed the children some time to absorb the demands of a game. At Hay Lane patience became immeasurable. It was not time spent waiting for a child to understand me; indeed it did not involve waiting at all. Patience had become the quality of being able to stay completely alive in the moment for however long that moment happened to be without desiring an outcome within a time frame. For me this has now become synonymous with acting.

Jacqui O'Hanlon, Head of Education at the RSC came to see my workshops at Hay Lane and I mentioned that I had always been interested in whether a scientific evaluation of these games would reveal their efficacy. Thanks to Jacqui, the RSC flew me over to Ohio State University and I played the games with children with autism, observed by Marc Tassé and his team at The Nisonger Center, as well as Lesley Ferris and her faculty from the theatre department. During that first visit I gave a workshop for which the Nisonger had invited young adults and their families to play with me for a two-hour session. A mother, father and their twenty-year-old son had made a long trip driving a few hundred miles to be there. The young man was amazing – picking up every game instantly and transforming himself into Caliban with an enthusiasm I had never seen before.

I'd become so used to working at Hay Lane where the majority of children were non-verbal that this young man reminded me how transformative the games can be at the higher end of the spectrum. I'd had to travel 3000 miles to truly discover the power of my own work and I confess I allowed myself a small sense of achievement and pride at the impact the games made that day. I was introduced to Robin Post on that first trip. We sat on a bench together before I left for the airport and I knew she was someone who understood what I had been trying to do. I let Jacqui and Lesley know that should my work be replicated in Ohio then Robin should run it. My radar for authenticity did not let me down; I doubt the project would have gone ahead without Robin, her humanity, talent and resolute hard work have single handedly allowed the research project to flourish.

I continue to work at Hay Lane School (now renamed The Village School). When the children see me, they instinctively place their hands to their hearts to make their 'Heartbeat hellos'. They have developed the habit of playing games of Shakespeare, the language has become embodied in their memories and they remember long phrases speaking them with facial and vocal expression. Although they experience profound struggles with learning they quote Shakespeare ad infinitum and seem to 'come to life' when doing so. The research project in Ohio may reveal why this is so and how far the positive effects may resonate. It will be interesting to see how important the art of playfulness is within the findings of the research and whether in fact playfulness is deemed measureable at all.

I've tried to convey the significance of playfulness within the games, but I'm not sure I'm any the wiser as to how to teach an actor, teacher or parent to *be* playful. It's a feeling born of personal experience, intimately related to growing up and deeply entrenched in our own unique personalities. My own sense of playfulness is to lose myself to fantasy, just as I used to in the wings of the Prince Edward Theatre when I was seventeen. It has also a good dose of truly not caring what others think, born out of my first-hand exposure to failure at nineteen. Having to think for myself, and indeed having the faith to outwardly change myself has, with hindsight, been playful – I seem to have spent my adult life emerging as the person I dreamed I could be. And I can see that having the faith to believe that a child with autism would 'throw me Bottom's donkey face' is truly playful, but it's only now that I analyse these actions in order to pass them on to others that I would name it so. The two worlds of Shakespeare and autism teach me more about myself than I could possibly pass on to others, perhaps that's playfulness too – a lifetime of self-schooling.

In his book *Far from the tree* Andrew Solomon says this: 'Some autistic people are optimistic and buoyant, and some are withdrawn and depressed; autism coincides with the full personality range to be found in the neurotypical population'. I would add that following on from this brilliantly simple observation is the conclusion that all children with autism are indeed children and all children deserve the chance to play.

Epilogue

It is with a bit of surprise, but with immense pleasure, that I find myself writing the epilogue to a book about Shakespeare and autism spectrum disorder (ASD). Up until three years ago, I had no idea I would be doing research in a theatre-based intervention with children with ASD. After hearing Kelly Hunter talk about her intervention and experience with children I became intrigued. This was only reinforced when I had the opportunity to observe Kelly do a demonstration with a small group of children with ASD. Although we use different words to describe the elements of the Hunter Heartbeat Method, I immediately saw many parallels between it and standardized social skills training programs I had done over the years. Woven into Kelly's intervention one finds transition activities, repetition, structure, predictability, didactic elements, modeling, role-playing, and retroactive feedback. All in a playful environment that provides multiple and varied opportunities to learn and practice skills that are not always easy to learn for children with autism spectrum disorder.

After several discussions and exchanges we agreed to collaborate on an initial pilot study of this intervention and embarked on an exciting inter-professional collaboration. Kelly worked with Robin Post and Lesley Ferris of the Ohio State University Department of Theatre to deliver the Hunter Heartbeat Method. Maggie Mehling and I from the Nisonger Center and Department of Psychology recruited a small team of research assistants to help organize the research environment for this efficacy study. An initial pilot study with 14 students with ASD yielded data indicating positive changes in the students' interpersonal skills, pragmatic language, and overall adaptive behavior after a ten-week intervention. The parents of the students who participated in this pilot study reported being surprised by the newly discovered interest in drama expressed by their sons and daughters and by the changes they observed by the end of the intervention. These initial pilot results were encouraging and have led to a larger intervention study with a better controlled design (waitlist control group and blinded assessors).

In conclusion, I was flattered when Kelly Hunter asked me to write this epilogue. I was especially pleased to learn that Kelly was putting to paper the 'games' and delivery method that she has developed over the years. This book will make possible taking the Hunter Heartbeat Method to any classroom, school, and agency where children with ASD play and learn.

Marc J. Tassé, PhD
Director, Nisonger Center
Professor of Psychology and Psychiatry
The Ohio State University

Index